A

Titles of publications are in *italics*

A8 countries migrants and homelessness 130.19
A-levels (Advanced Level) 139.4
   'dumbing down' claims 139.19–20
   and gender 139.10
   results 139.18
   science 139.21
AACTP (Alcohol Attention Control Training
     Programme) 143.39
abdominal obesity, health risks 113.11, 15
abductions by terrorists 92.9
abortion
   access to abortions 126.24
   after-effects 126.10, 11, 14
   arguments against (pro-life) 126.21–2, 25
   arguments for (pro-choice) 126.21
   clinics 126.12
   confidentiality 126.13, 28, 29, 30
   costs 126.12
   deaths from 20.25, 27, 30
   decision-making 126.9–10, 12–13
     men 126.15–16
     young people 126.17–18
   and depression 126.11
   early medical abortion 126.14, 33
   and emergency contraception (the morning after
     pill) 126.24
   ethical considerations 126.21–2
   and fetal abnormality 126.9, 34, 35
   home abortions 126.32–4
   and humanism 126.4–5
   late abortion 126.14, 37–8
   and the law 126.5, 6, 7–8, 12
   and men 126.15–16
   methods
     medical abortion ('the abortion pill') 126.10,
      14, 32–4
     vacuum aspiration ('the suction method') 126.10,
      14
   reasons for abortions 126.8, 9, 21
     fetal abnormality 126.9, 34, 35
     late abortions 126.37
   religious positions on 126.1–3, 6
   risks 126.10, 14
     home abortions 126.32, 34
   statistics 126.18
   and teenage pregnancies 20.30, 34; 126.29; 133.2, 9
     under 16s 126.13, 28, 29; 133.2
   time limit 126.12, 36–8
Abortion Act 126.6, 8, 12
Abortion Law Reform Association 126.7
abrupt climate change 95.17–20
absenteeism 107.6–8, 18
   and obesity 113.17
abuse as cause of self-harm 136.1
abusers *see* child abusers
academic achievement *see* educational achievement
academic freedom 121.8–9

academies 139.14
   Special Educational Needs provision 135.36
Acceptable Behaviour Contract 137.35
access, disabled people 135.3
   and Disability Discrimination Act 135.22
access courses 139.30
access rights, fathers 133.39
Accession 8 (A8) migrants and homelessness 130.19
accident warning devices, cars 119.19
accidents
   alcohol-related 123.16
   child labour and work-related 99.1
   compensation, and same-sex partnerships 101.30–1
   and older people 105.5
   road accidents, children 119.5, 28, 30–31
   and young travellers 109.12, 14–15
achievement *see* educational achievement
acid rain 76.11
acne 123.28
ActionAid 98.28–9, 30
active euthanasia 102.1, 2
active traffic management 119.37–8
activists and the media 142.10
activity
   as help for depression 125.3, 39
   and improving self-esteem 117.6, 8, 33
   physical *see* exercise
Acts of Parliament 131.24
acupressure 81.1, 3
acupuncture 81.5–6, 14, 23, 36
addictions 123.8; 141.9–10
   cannabis 128.2, 8, 15
   gambling *see* compulsive gambling
   drugs 114.5, 17–18
   to the Internet 142.37
   nicotine 123.12; 145.26
   children 145.2–3
   to self-harm 136.9
   shopping 134.13–14
   signs 123.14
addictiveness of gambling 129.30
ADD *see* attention deficit disorder
ADHD (attention deficit and hyperactivity disorder)
     141.19
   and eating disorders 127.10
administration method and drug effects 114.2
admissions, school, gender equality 112.9
adoption
   as alternative to abortion 126.24
   and children's rights 120.11
   and father's rights 133.39
   process 133.8–9
adrenaline and nicotine 145.26
adult children
   parental interference 124.14–15
   supported by parents 124.3
adult deaths from AIDS, impact on children 110.37
adult literacy rates, and child labour 99.11–12
adultescents 124.3
adults
   consequences of childhood abuse 132.6

consequences of childhood bullying **122**.6
    participation in sports **118**.1
advance directives (living wills) **102**.18, 29, 32, 33–9
advance fee scams **134**.26–7
Advanced Extension Awards (AEA) **139**.18
Advanced Highers **139**.4
adventure travel **109**.9–10
advertising **134**.7–1
    anti-smoking **145**.18–19
    benefits of **134**.9
    and body image **117**.18
    and children **134**.10, 12
    cigarettes
        and children **145**.2
        EU ban **145**.7
    and drinking behaviour, young people **143**.17, 19, 20
    junk food **88**.10, 11, 19, 20, 35, 37
        and childhood obesity **113**.2
    regulation **134**.7,10
    and sex discrimination **112**.14
Advertising Standards Authority (ASA) **134**.7, 10
aerobic exercise **113**.22
aerosol cans recycling **111**.36
affirmation and self-confidence **117**.34
affluence *see* wealth
affluenza **134**.5
affordable housing **85**.29–31
    and the exception site policy **85**.28
    giving public money to private developers **85**.19
    Government strategies **130**.16, 33
    and housing associations **85**.19
    large houses **85**.11
    policies **85**.28–30
    and public sector workers **85**.1, 3, 4, 20, 21, 22
    in rural areas **85**.5, 28, 31
    shortage of **85**.1, 3, 8–9, 20; **130**.8, 23
    and social housing **85**.8
    and young workers **85**.3–4
Africa
    cannabis production **128**.24
    and genetically modified crops **138**.23
    ideal female body shape **117**.30
    poverty **110**.31, 32
African–Caribbean people **115**.5
    pupils, exclusion **115**.19
African Movement for Working Children **120**.19–20
Akwaaba (Barnardo's project) **114**.28
America, cannabis production **128**.24
Amos, Baroness Valerie **115**.16
age
    and adventure travel **109**.9
    and alcohol consumption **123**.16–17; **143**.2, 17, 29
    and breast cancer **60**.23
    and child labour **99**.2
    and child soldiers **99**.29–30
    of children and divorcing parents **106**.33–4;
        124.33–4
    and children's rights **120**.1,2
    of criminal responsibility **120**.12; **137**.11, 13
    of divorce **106**.3, 23, 25, 26
    and drinking behaviour, young people **143**.16

    and effects of alcohol **143**.7
    of first cohabitation **106**.10
    of first drink **143**.16, 21
    of first sexual intercourse **133**.1
    and first-time house buyers **85**.7
    of homeless people **130**.10, 14
    and Internet safety **104**.22–3
    and Internet shopping **104**.7
    and Internet use **104**.12
    of lone parents **106**.3
    of marriage **106**.3, 25
    of retirement **105**.20, 27
    and sale of tobacco **145**.3
    of self-harmers **136**.4, 20
    of smokers **145**.1
    and stress levels **100**.13
    and suicidal intent **136**.26
    victims of crime **137**.4
    and voter turnout **131**.19
    voting age lowering **120**.7–8; **131**.28, 29, 30
    and worry about violent crime **137**.7
    of young offenders **137**.14
age of consent **99**.25–6; **101**.27; **133**.1
age discrimination **110**.19–20
    see also ageism
age ratings
    films **121**.23–5, 29–30
    video games **121**.32–3
age-related macular degeneration **144**.22
ageing
    benefits of exercise **113**.22
    genetic engineering and the postponement of
        105.31–3
    and the longevity revolution **105**.35–6
ageing population **20**.4, 5, 9, 33
    in developing countries **20**.9, 11
    and the pension crisis **105**.19, 25, 26
    and replacement migration **20**.15, 16
    services for the **20**.34–5
    statistics **105**.4, 19
ageism
    and employment **105**.4, 16–27
    and health discrimination **105**.17
    legislation on age discrimination **105**.18, 20, 23–4,
        26
    and older women **105**.16, 21–2
    and young people **105**.16, 24
Agenda 21 **111**.3
aggression, encouraged by corporal punishment **132**.10
agriculture
    and bioenergy **97**.18
    and child labour **99**.1, 2, 4
    and climate change **95**.3, 7, 9, 11, 12, 14, 15, 25, 26
    coffee growers **98**.13, 17
    cotton farming **98**.24
    egg production **140**.38–9
    energy crops **95**.29
    exotic animals **140**.30
    farm-retail price gap **98**.28
    and food nutrition **88**.31–4
    free trade in agriculture **88**.33

Issues
Annual Index
2007

ISSUES

Compiled by
Ann Shooter

Independence
Educational Publishers
Cambridge

Volume numbers appear first (in bold) followed by page numbers; a change in volume number is preceded by a semi-colon.

Vol. **20** Population Growth
Vol. **22** Confronting Child Abuse
Vol. **29** Gambling
Vol. **43** A Consumer Society
Vol. **60** Confronting Cancer
Vol. **69** The Media
Vol. **74** Money Matters
Vol. **75** Lone-Parent Families
Vol. **76** The Water Crisis
Vol. **77** Self-inflicted Violence
Vol. **78** Threatened Species
Vol. **79** Dealing with Homelessness
Vol. **80** The Cannabis Debate
Vol. **81** Alternative Therapies
Vol. **82** Protecting our Privacy
Vol. **83** Dealing with Crime
Vol. **84** Mental Wellbeing
Vol. **85** The Housing Crisis
Vol. **86** Smoking and your Health
Vol. **87** Genetic Modification
Vol. **88** Food and Nutrition
Vol. **89** Refugees
Vol. **90** Human and Animal Cloning
Vol. **91** Disability Issues
Vol. **92** Terrorism
Vol. **93** Binge Drinking
Vol. **94** Religions and Beliefs in Britain

Vol. **95** The Climate Crisis
Vol. **96** Preventing Sexual Diseases
Vol. **97** Energy Matters
Vol. **98** The Globalisation Issue
Vol. **99** Exploited Children
Vol. **100** Stress and Anxiety
Vol. **101** Sexuality and Discrimination
Vol. **102** The Ethics of Euthanasia
Vol. **103** Animal Rights
Vol. **104** Our Internet Society
Vol. **105** Ageing Issues
Vol. **106** Trends in Marriage
Vol. **107** Work Issues
Vol. **108** Domestic Violence
Vol. **109** Responsible Tourism
Vol. **110** Poverty
Vol. **111** The Waste Problem
Vol. **112** Women, Men and Equality
Vol. **113** Fitness and Health
Vol. **114** Drug Abuse
Vol. **115** Racial Discrimination
Vol. **116** Grief and Loss
Vol. **117** Self-Esteem and Body Image
Vol. **118** Focus on Sport
Vol. **119** Transport Trends
Vol. **120** The Human Rights Issue
Vol. **121** The Censorship Debate

Vol. **122** Bullying
Vol. **123** Young People and Health
Vol. **124** Parenting Issues
Vol. **125** Understanding Depression
Vol. **126** The Abortion Debate
Vol. **127** Eating Disorders
Vol. **128** The Cannabis Issue
Vol. **129** Gambling Trends
Vol. **130** Homelessness
Vol. **131** Citizenship and National Identity
Vol. **132** Child Abuse
Vol. **133** Teen Pregnancy and Lone Parents
Vol. **134** Customers and Consumerism
Vol. **135** Coping with Disability
Vol. **136** Self-harm
Vol. **137** Crime and Anti-Social Behaviour
Vol. **138** A Genetically Modified Future?
Vol. **139** The Education Problem
Vol. **140** Vegetarian and Alternative Diets
Vol. **141** Mental Health and Wellbeing
Vol. **142** Media Issues
Vol. **143** Problem Drinking
Vol. **144** The Cloning Debate
Vol. **145** Smoking Trends

and global water shortages **76**.3, 4, 8
and globalisation **98**.5–6, 15–16
land degradation **20**.3, 8, 9, 13, 14, 23, 24
and new house-building **85**.28, 33
and population growth **20**.1, 8
subsidies **98**.10, 17
and water management **76**.18, 36
and water pollution **76**.11
WTO trade rules **98**.21
see also animal welfare; food production; genetically
    modified (GM) crops; organic farming
agrifood TNCs **98**.28–9, 30
agro-chemicals **138**.4
aid **98**.3; **110**.28
    public opinions on **110**.34
AIDS (Acquired Immune Deficiency Syndrome) **96**.7,
    17–22, 36–9
and child labour **99**.3
and child soldiers **99**.31
effect on children **110**.37
deaths from **96**.36
and dementia **141**.7
in developing countries **20**.20, 34
education programmes **96**.32
global funding **96**.39
global statistics **96**.17–18, 24, 30, 36, 38
and medical research **103**.12, 13
orphans **96**.39
pandemic **96**.31
and parents of lesbians and gays **101**.17
and population growth **20**.3, 5, 7, 11
prevention programmes **20**.25, 27, 28, 30, 37
and the sexual exploitation of children **99**.24
tackling stigma and discrimination **96**.19, 39
treatments **96**.18, 20
    antiretroviral therapy (ART) **96**.36, 37, 38, 39
    fixed dose combinations (FDCs) **96**.37
    vaccines **96**.33–4
UK statistics **96**.20–2
and young people **96**.24–6, 29
see also HIV (Human Immunodeficiency Virus)
air pollution **95**.27
    and transport **119**.1, 15, 16, 31
air travel
airport surveillance **120**.34
carbon dioxide emissions from **97**.25
disabled people **135**.9
and global tourism **109**.2
and global warming **109**.19
and pollution **119**.16
and privacy rights **82**.3
and responsible tourism **109**.18
and terrorism
    basic advice **92**.39
    fear of **92**.3, 4, 13
    prohibited items **92**.39
    security measures **92**.32
terrorist attacks using aircraft **92**.9, 11
and UK travel trends **109**.4
women pilots **112**.27
al-Qaeda **92**.2, 8, 9, 11, 12, 14, 17–18; **94**.10

and counter-terrorism in the UK **92**.30, 34
and bin Laden **92**.18
media coverage of **92**.23
and suicide attacks **92**.16
training camps **92**.18
alcohol **88**.7, 24; **114**.4; **123**.14–19
and accidents **123**.16
advertising, effects on young people **143**.17, 19, 20
Alcohol Harm Reduction Strategy **143**.37
alcopops **143**.1, 3
beer **143**.1
and brain function
calories in **143**.2
and cancer **60**.1, 15
consumption
    children **143**.20
    older people **143**.9–10, 30
    regional variations **143**.13
    worldwide increase **143**.5
    young people **123**.1–2, 9, 18–19; **143**.2, 5, 15, 20,
        37
daily benchmarks **143**.8, 25, 26–7, 34
    awareness of **143**.11, 34
deaths related to **143**.3, 6, 37
and depression **125**.2, 3, 36–7
drinks industry and responsible drinking **143**.27
and drugs **114**.16, 17; **143**.3, 10
effects of **123**.15–16, 18; **125**.37; **143**.3, 7, 23
as food weakness **113**.14
health benefits of **143**.4, 7, 27
health risks of **143**.6, 9–10
and the law **114**.31; **143**.2–3
    young people **143**.2, 17
    see also drink-driving
licences **143**.2
and life expectancy **105**.2, 9–10, 29, 31; **143**.13
and mental health **141**.34
and pregnancy **143**.3, 25, 27, 33–4
purchasing **143**.11
    underage **143**.16, 17, 20, 28
and religion **94**.10
responsible drinking **143**.26–7, 29
risks
    of alcohol consumption **143**.3, 21–2
    of binge drinking **143**.4, 15
    in pregnancy **143**.3, 33
as self-medication for mental health problems
    125.36–7
spirits **143**.1
strength **123**.16; **143**.1, 10
and stress **100**.27, 31, 37, 39
support groups **123**.17; **143**.38, 39
and television **143**.18–19, 20
trends **143**.1–24
UK legislation on the sale of **114**.31; **143**.2
underage drinking **125**.9; **137**.14; **143**.16, 20, 28
    see also young people and alcohol
units of **143**.1, 26
    awareness of **143**.11
    drink labelling **143**.30, 32
and violence **137**.8

wine
    health benefits **143**.4
    strength **143**.1
  see also binge drinking; young people and alcohol
alcohol abuse **143**.25–39
  costs of **143**.36
  government strategies **143**.36–7
  and homeless people **130**.11, 12, 20
  and older people **105**.38; **143**.9–10, 30
  risks **143**.3, 4, 9, 13, 14
  signs of **143**.25, 35
  statistics **143**.37
  street drinking **130**.12
  treatment **143**.35, 38–9
  young people **143**.29, 37
  see also underage drinking
Alcohol Attention Training Programme **143**.39
Alcoholics Anonymous **143**.39
alcolocks **119**.8–9
alcopops **143**.1, 3
allergens, definition of **138**.4
alternative burials **116**.36, 38
aluminium recycling **111**.11, 23–4, 26
Alzheimer's disease **105**.3, 29, 37; **141**.6
  and animal experimentation **144**.34
  diagnosis using eye test **141**.19
  and diet **125**.12
amenorrhea **113**.23
American Civil War **92**.7
amino acids **140**.7, 23
amnesia **141**.11
amphibians
  and evolution **78**.1
  and the exotic pet trade **78**.21
anabolic agents/steroids **114**.29
  and the law **114**.32; **118**.35, 36
anaesthesia, and animal experiments **103**.6, 8, 9, 12, 22
analgesics **114**.29
Anarchist terrorist groups **92**.7
Anatomy of Hell film **121**.24
Ancient Greece, sport and drugs **118**.23
Andrea Adams Trust **122**.32
androstenedione (andro) **118**.35
anger
  and bereavement **116**.4, 8, 19
  dealing with **136**.3
  and sexual abuse, dealing with **132**.28
  and traumatic bereavement **116**.11
anger management **108**.2
  for bullies **122**.18
Anglicanism **94**.1
  see also Church of England
angling **103**.30
  and mental well-being **117**.38
animal cloning **144**.30–39
  Dolly the sheep **144**.1, 15, 30–31, 32, 34, 39
  and factory farming **144**.35
  and food production **144**.36–9
  and milk production **144**.36–8, 39
  risks **144**.39
animal cruelty **103**.32–9

and abuse **103**.32
and animal welfare law **103**.33–5
education in preventing **103**.35
and the fur trade **103**.36–9
statistics **103**.34–5
animal experiments **103**.1–23
  alternatives to **103**.7, 9, 10, 13–14, 17–19, 22, 23
  clinical studies **103**.7, 18, 22
  computer research **103**.13–14, 17, 19, 22
  epidemiology (population studies) **103**.17, 18, 19, 22
  reasons for not using **103**.19
  reasons for using **103**.19
  tissue and cell cultures **103**.14, 17–18, 19, 22
  and animal rights activists **103**.2, 9
  and the anti-vivisection belief system **103**.22–3
  arguments against **103**.2, 5–7; **144**.34
  arguments for **103**.2, 9
  benefits of in scientific research **103**.3
  cosmetic testing **103**.23
  and cruelty **103**.6–7, 9, 22
  and fears of endangering patients **103**.21
  and genetic research **103**.11
  and genetically modified animals **103**.1, 8; **144**.34
  and humanism **140**.32–3
  and the law **103**.16, 20
  and medical advances **103**.10–11
  and moral justification **103**.7
  questions and answers on **103**.10–11
  regulation of **103**.1–2, 16, 20, 21
  replacement of **103**.9
  statistics **103**.1, 4, 8
  and toxicological procedures **103**.8, 10
  types of animals used in **103**.1, 5–6, 8, 22
  unreliability of **103**.6
  and veterinary research **103**.10
animal fat as food ingredient **140**.18
animal feed **88**.35–6
  GM content **138**.25, 26
animal-human embryos **144**.9, 11, 13, 14, 20
animal rights **103**.32–3
animal rights activists
  and animal experiments **103**.2, 9, 11
  Government policies on **103**.23
  laws against **103**.15–16
animal sentience **140**.27–8
animal suffering **140**.32
animal welfare **88**.32–3, 35–6; **140**.27–39
  consumer attitudes **140**.14, 31, 33
  egg production **140**.38–9
  Freedom Food mark **140**.34
  And humanism **140**.31–3
  meat production **140**.13
  organic farms **140**.35–6
  UK legislation on **121**.7
animals
  and climate change **95**.3, 9, 11, 14–15
  endangered species **95**.22
  extinction of species **95**.1, 9, 14, 15, 26, 38
  in the UK **95**.27
  Muslim views of **92**.26
anniversaries and grief **116**.20

anorexia nervosa **123**.7, 33–4; **127**.1, 11–12
  as auto-immune disease **127**.12
  children and young people **127**.20
Anti-Bullying Alliance **122**.7
anti-bullying practices
  schools **122**.18, 25
  workplaces **122**.39
anti-capitalism **98**.2
anti-depressant drugs **125**.24–5, 32
  and adolescents **125**.8, 27
  and children **123**.28; **125**.27
  and ecstasy **114**.16
  and postnatal depression **125**.18
  and seasonal affective disorder **125**.38
  and young people **123**.28
  see also drug treatments for depression
anti-doping initiatives **118**.25–8
  international **118**.27–8, 31–2
  UK **118**. 26–7, 28, 30
anti-gay taunts, football **118**.17
anti-obesity campaign, influence on children's body
    image **117**.22
anti-psychotic drugs **125**.19
anti-racism
  and football **118**.14
  laws *see* legislation and racism
anti-social behaviour
  adults unwilling to intervene **137**.26, 27
  and homelessness **130**.7
  impact of interventions **137**.35
  by young people **137**.17
  young people's concerns about **137**.24
Anti-Social Behaviour Act 2003 **120**.12
Anti-Social Behaviour Orders (ASBOs) **137**.4, 12,
    21–3, 35
anti-social driving habits **119**.9
anti-terrorism measures
  and deportation **120**.38–9
  and identity cards **120**.35
  Muslims' views on **115**.34
antibiotics **88**.14
  development of **105**.2
  and medical research **103**.12
  and organic farming **140**.35
  resistance to **138**.4
  and genetically modified organisms **138**.13
antiretroviral therapy (ART) **96**.36, 37, 38, 39
anxiety
  and childhood depression **125**.28
  dangers of severe **100**.21
  defining **100**.21
  and depression **100**.24
  and stress **100**.2, 21
  symptoms of **100**.21
appearance, effects of smoking **145**.30–31
appetite-suppressing hormones **127**.38–9
Applied AS awards **139**.18
apprenticeships **107**.36
aquifers, and global water supplies **76**.7, 16, 19
Arctic ice-cap melting **95**.3, 7, 8, 24, 33, 38
armed conflict

and the sexual exploitation of children **99**.20–1
  war-affected children **99**.32–3
  see also child soldiers
armed forces
  homeless ex-servicemen **130**.11
  and homosexuality **101**.25–6, 29, 32
  recruitment age **120**.20
  suicide of soldiers, Japan **136**.39
aromatherapy **81**.23, 36
  and cancer **81**.10, 33
  and multiple sclerosis **81**.30
  questions and answers **81**.10
  and scientists **81**.28, 29
  and stress relief **100**.37
arranged marriages **106**.15–18
arrests
  for drug use **114**.36; **128**.11
  your rights **128**.35–6
  of young offenders **137**.7
arts-in-health movement **141**.38
arts therapies **141**.38
artwork as way of remembrance **116**.16
AS-levels (Advanced Supplementary levels) **139**.4, 18
asbestos recycling **111**.35
ASBOs (Anti-Social Behaviour Orders) **137**.4, 12,
    21–3, 35
Asian people
  Asian-British women and body image **117**.29
  British identity **115**.37
  footballers **118**.13, 15–16
Asians Can't Play Football report **118**.15
Asperger's syndrome **135**.34
aspirations gap **107**.2
Assassins (eleventh-century Islamic terrorists) **92**.1, 6, 7
assault on children **120**.14–15
  in detention centres **120**.17
assertiveness training **117**.3
  and stress **100**.32
assessment, educational and gender equality **112**.11
assisted dying bill, and disability rights **135**.24
assisted suicide
  defining **102**.1
  and disabled people **135**.24
  humanist view on **102**.1–2
  and the law **102**.5
  in Britain **102**.7, 8, 11, 15–16, 17, 20
  international comparisons **102**.7, 15
  public attitudes to **102**.9, 10, 17, 18, 27
  questions and answers on **102**.3–5
  and the right-to-die movement **102**.18–19
  safeguards **102**.2, 31
  'slippery slope' argument against **102**.2
  statistics **102**.17
  see also physician-assisted suicide (PAS)
asthma
  increasing **119**.13, 26, 31
  and passive smoking **145**.28, 29
asylum seekers **120**.31
  in Britain *see* Britain, asylum seekers
  children **120**.21–2
  conditions for granting refugee status **89**.1

fleeing from conflict **89**.7–8
and HIV **96**.39
and homelessness **130**.11–12, 19
and housing **85**.2, 13
illegal immigration and identity cards **82**.2, 7, 8, 9, 10, 11
numbers of **89**.2, 5, 6, 10
top asylum nationalities **89**.1–2, 5, 6, 10
top countries receiving **89**.2, 5, 10
see also refugees
atheism **94**.7, 15
athletics and drugs *see* drugs in sport
Atkins diet, effect on eating habits **113**.14
attempted suicide **136**.27–8
and gender **136**.33
and homophobia **101**.22
and the law **102**.4, 5
and stress in young people **100**.4
Attendance Allowance **135**.5
attention deficit disorder (ADD) **127**.7
and eating disorders **127**.10
attention deficit and hyperactivity disorder (ADHD) **141**.19
and eating disorders **127**.10
attention-seeking and self-harm **136**.2–3, 8
auctions and consumer rights **134**.20
authoritarian parenting style **124**.8; **132**.18
authoritative parenting style **124**.8; **132**.18
autism **135**.34
auto-immune disease, anorexia as **127**.12
Aynsley-Green, Al, Children's Commissioner **122**.7, 17

babies
and HIV **96**.31, 39
killing of newborn **102**.25–6
and mother's smoking **145**.32–3
and poverty **110**.11
see also infant mortality
Bach flowers **81**.1
Bacillus cereus **88**.29
Bacillus thuringiensis (Bt) cotton **138**.35
backpackers
global nomads **109**.10
and insurance **109**.14–15
bacteria **88**.27, 28–9
transgenic **144**.11
baculoviruses **138**.13–14
Balance of Good Health food guide **113**.32
balanced diet *see* healthy eating
Balkan wars **89**.15
banks
basic bank accounts **74**.18, 24
children and bank accounts **74**.6–7, 13
current accounts **74**.18–19, 24
financial education programmes for schools **74**.13
Internet banking **74**.2, **104**.12
and pharming **104**.33–4
and phishing **104**.32–3

and money management **106**.14
overdrafts **74**.1, 18, 19, 21–2, 37
savings accounts **74**.13, 19, 24
and students **74**.2, 17, 21–2
and young people **74**.9, 17–19
Barnardo's help for families in poverty **110**.5
BASF GM potato trials **138**.27–8
Basque separatists **92**.2, 19
batteries, recycling **111**.31, 35
battery eggs
supermarket bans **140**.38
see also free range eggs
Bayer CropScience, GM rice **138**.20, 31–4
BBC
funding **142**.6
Not Seen, not Heard report **135**.35
Be the FULL STOP campaign **132**.5–6
bed and breakfast hotels and older people **130**.18
beer
strength **143**.1
and young people **123**.1
Befrienders Worldwide website **136**.32
begging **130**.12
children as beggars **99**.3, 4
giving to beggars **130**.32
behaviour
effects of cannabis use **128**.16
effects of child abuse **132**.23
gender differences **112**.28, 32–3, 35
and healthy self-esteem **117**.30
and low self-esteem **117**.5
problems in schools **120**.16
stress and behavioural changes **100**.33
symptoms of workplace bullying **122**.31
Benefit Agency **135**.6
Benefit Enquiry Line **135**.6
benefits *see* state benefits
benefits of globalisation **98**.1, 12
benzene emissions, traffic **119**.15
bereavement **116**.1–18
children *see* children and bereavement
counselling **116**.6
feelings **116**.1, 3–4, 5, 7–9, 10–11, 19, 21–2, 30
help from GP **116**.2
by murder **116**.8
and stress in young people **100**.2
by suicide **116**.8
support **116**.2, 14–15
beta-blockers **118**.37
betting **129**.2
see also gambling
Beyond Compare Photo Tour **117**.13
bias and the media **142**.10
Big Issue, The **130**.33, 37
BIG recycle **111**.25
bigorexia **127**.19
bilateral trade agreements **98**.10
bill payments
and direct debit **74**.9, 23
and young people **74**.2, 23
Bills (parliamentary) **131**.24

binge buying **134**.13, 14
binge drinking **143**.4, 13, 14
    children **143**.20
    Europe **143**.31
    older people **143**.9–10, 30
    parents' worries about **124**.17
    risks **143**.4, 14
    young people **143**.5, 15
binge eating **127**.2, 15–16
bingo **129**.2
biodegradable plastics **111**.23
biodegradable waste **111**.3
biodiesel vehicles **119**.21
biodiversity
    and endangered animals **78**.6
    framework for measuring **78**.27
    hot spots and population growth **20**.21
    loss of freshwater **76**.35
biodynamic massage **81**.1
bioenergy **97**.18
    biofuels **97**.9; **138**.4
    biomass **95**.34; **97**.5, 6, 9, 11, 18
biological effects of compulsive gambling **129**.29
biology and gender development **112**.28
biometrics **120**.33–4
Biosafety Protocol **138**.19, 27
biotechnology
    definition **138**.4
    public attitudes to **138**.15–16; **144**.19
bipolar affective disorder (manic depression) **125**.2, 4,
       10, 19–20; **141**.14–15
    defining **125**.19
    experiences of sufferers **141**.28–9
    symptoms **125**.19
    treatments **125**.19–20
birth control, teenagers **123**.22–3
    awareness of birth control services **123**.3
    see also contraception
birth country, non–white ethnic groups **115**.38
    UK as birth country **131**.8
birth rates
    births outside marriage **106**.4; **124**.22
    in developing countries **20**.1–2, 10, 38
    fall in **20**.4, 8, 16, 26, 36, 38; **106**.2
    and population ageing **20**.15
    to teenage mothers **133**.2
    see also teenage pregnancies
bisexuals **101**.1, 2, 4, 9, 11, 38
    issues facing young women **101**.19–20
    parents of **101**.17
black box for road charging **119**.36
black people
    educational performance of children **115**.19–20
    pupils **115**.18–21; **139**.9
    women, body image **117**.29, 30
    see also employment and racism; ethnic minorities;
      racism
Black Pupils' Achievement Programme **115**.20
bladder cancer **60**.16, 17
bladder repair, stem cell therapy **144**.21
blame, feelings of

following bereavement **116**.8, 11, 19
    and low self-esteem **117**.6
blasphemy laws **94**.37, 39; **121**.16
    and cartoons of Mohammed **121**.12
blended families **124**.39
blogs **142**.37
blood cholesterol levels and exercise **113**.34
blood doping **118**.38
blood pressure *see* high blood pressure (hypertension)
blood products, and HIV **96**.14
blood sugar levels **88**.15
    and binge eating **127**.15
blood tests for diagnosing mental illness **141**.18
blue badge scheme (disabled people) **135**.7–8
BMA (British Medical Association) views on abortion
    126.22
BMI *see* body mass index
boardroom positions, women **112**.18
body dysmorphic disorder/dysmorphophobia **127**.18–19
body image **117**.10–30
    assessment of **117**.18
    boys **117**.23
    and eating disorders **127**.27
    and ethnicity **117**.29–30
    and exercise **141**.39
    girls **117**.19, 20–21, 22, 25
    improving **117**.10–11, 15, 18–19
    and the media **117**.11–12, 15, 17–18; **127**.23, 25–6, 27
    negative
        girls **117**.25
        teenage girls **117**.20–22
        women **117**.14–15
    positive **117**.10
    and self-esteem **117**.10–11
    study **127**.29
    women **117**.19
        confidence about **112**.31
        and ethnicity **117**.29–30
        and media pressure **117**.11–12, 14–15
        timeline **117**.16–17
body language and avoiding bullying **122**.5
body mass index (BMI) **88**.8; **113**.9, 11, 31; **127**.32
    measurement, children **127**.36
body shapes **127**.22
    effect of smoking **145**.31
body weight **88**.1, 12, 18
    and exercise **113**.34, 39
    and smoking **145**.30–31
    see also obesity; weight management
BodyTalk workshops **117**.13
Bolivia, privatisation of water services **110**.22
bombing attacks **92**.9, 11
bonded labour **120**.29
bone cancer **60**.9, 11, 35
bone density, effects of eating disorders **127**.5
bone marrow stem cells
    and heart disease treatment **144**.23
    and sperm cell creation **144**.29
bone marrow transplants **60**.35, 36; **144**.24
books and portrayal of disabled children **135**.21
border controls **89**.20

borrowing *see* debt
bottles
    plastic **111**.26–7
    reusing 23
Bourne Judgement **126**.7–8
bowel cancer **60**.3, 4, 6, 14, 16
boys and young men
    academic performance **112**.1, 8, 11
    ambivalence towards girls **112**.34
    and body image **117**.23
    and careers in childcare **112**.23
    and child labour **99**.2
    child soldiers **99**.31, 36
    and eating disorders **123**.33
    and education
        foundation stage **112**.7
        single-sex teaching **112**.5–6
        underachievement **112**.3
    and gender equality **112**.33–4
    and Internet access **104**.3
    and mental health problems **141**.1
    and non-traditional jobs **112**.21
    and parenthood **133**.25–7
    and puberty **127**.22
    self-harm **136**.7
    sexual exploitation of **99**.16, 21
    and smoking **145**.2, 5
    street children **99**.19
BPAS (British Pregnancy Advisory Service) **126**.7
Bradford, education of ethnic minority children **115**.33
brain
    effects of alcohol on **125**.37; **143**.4
    effects of cannabis on **128**.34
    effect of diet **141**.30–31
    effect of nicotine **145**.25, 26
    stem cell therapy for brain damage **144**.22
brain cancer **60**.5
brain tumours in children **60**.9, 10, 12
Brake (road safety charity) **114**.23–4
brand awareness, children **134**.11
brand image and advertising **134**.8–9
brand names as children's names **134**.12
brat-bullies **122**.9–10
breakfast, importance of **127**.23
breakfast clubs **123**.31
breast cancer **60**.3, 4, 24–5
    and age **60**.23
    and breast awareness **60**.18, 22
    and complementary therapies **81**.23
    and men **60**.22
    and radiotherapy **60**.37
    screening programme **60**.13, 22, 23
    and smoking **60**.16
    survival rates **60**.4, 6, 13, 14, 27
    treatment **60**.4, 35
breast surgery, teenagers **117**.26–8
Breathing Space advice line **136**.34
bring site **111**.3
Bristol University, workplace travel plan **119**.32–3
Britain, asylum seekers
    appeals process **89**.13–14, 29, 33

asylum claims procedure **89**.12, 13–14
asylum legislation **89**.11, 12, 33, 39
citizenship acceptance **89**.37
costs of the asylum system **89**.11, 30
detention centres **89**.12, 13
health treatment **89**.19–20
legal aid **89**.29
number of asylum claims **89**.16, 18, 23
refused asylum applications **89**.11, 13–14, 18
welfare support **89**.12, 13, 14, 19, 30, 38
Britain, gender gap ranking **112**.29
Britain, poverty **110**.1–20
    child poverty **110**.4, 5, 6–7
    income inequality **110**.13, 14, 16
British Board of Film Classification (BBFC) **121**.22, 23–5
British Crime Survey **137**.3
British history, importance of teaching **131**.7
British identity 1–14
    Asians **115**.37
    and non-white ethnic groups **115**.38
    see also Britishness
British Medical Association (BMA), views on abortion **126**.22
British Pregnancy Advisory Service (BPAS) **126**.7
British population
    ethnic groups **115**.3
    mixed-race relationships **115**.24
British tourists
    and adventure travel **109**.9–10
    and independent holidays **109**.8-9
British Youth Council **131**.33
    and lowering voting age **131**.28
Britishness **131**.1–14
    decline of **131**.9
    effect of devolution **131**.5, 6
    and Islamophobia **131**.11
    and multiculturalism **131**.10
    see also British identity
broadband services **104**.3
broadcasting
    illegal **142**.7
    mergers **142**.4
    see also radio; television
Broadcasting Code **121**.36
Broadcasting Complaints Commission (BCC) **121**.36
broadcasting regulation **121**.36–7
broadsheet newspapers **142**.8
Brook Advisory Centres **96**.13; **101**.3, 4
brownfield sites
    and agricultural land **85**.28
    decontaminating **85**.22
    and new house-building **85**.9, 26, 34
    and wildlife in London **85**.16–17
BSE (bovine spongiform encephalopathy)
    and freedom of information **88**.14
Bt cotton **138**.35
BTecs, impact of specialist diplomas **139**.23–4
Buckinghamshire County Council, workplace travel plan **119**.32
Buddhism **94**.6, 19, 21

abortion and contraception **126**.3
  beliefs **94**.2, 4
  and the Census (2001) **94**.3, 5, 28
  festivals **94**.4
  food rules **94**.10
  funerals **116**.35
  Golden Rule **94**.8, 11
  and RE (religious education) **94**.9
budgeting
  and students **74**.2, 28, 30, 32
  and young people **74**.2, 3, 14–15, 23
building industry, and energy efficiency **97**.36
building waste recycling **111**.35
Bulger, James, murder case **137**.13
bulimia nervosa **123**.7; **127**.1–2, 13–14
  children and young people **127**.20
bullies
  anger management training **122**.18
  how to stop bullying **122**.2, 9–10
  no-blame policy **122**.6–7
  reasons for bullying **122**.8–9
bullying **122**.1–39
  bullying behaviour **122**.8, 9–10, 15–16
  Bullying Online helpline **122**.6
  cyber-bullying **122**.19–26
  definition **122**.1, 5, 8
  extent of **122**.11, 17, 22–3
  responding to bullying **122**.1–2, 5–6, 13, 16; **123**.3
  cyber-bullying **122**.19, 20, 21, 23, 24
  workplace bullying **122**.27, 31–2, 33, 37–8
  homophobic **101**.3, 13, 18, 19, 20, 21–2, 38–9
  reasons for **122**.8–9
  and sexual harassment **112**.11
  and stress in young people **100**.1, 2, 4
  types of bullying **122**.15–116, 18
  at work **122**.27–39
  and workplace stress **100**.14, 15
  and young people **122**.1–18
  see also bullies; racist bullying; school bullying;
    workplace bullying
burial **116**.37–9
  alternative burials **116**.36, 38
  natural **134**.31
  on private land **116**.39
  at sea **116**.39
burns, first aid **136**.23
burying bad news **121**.17–18
bus travel
  and disabled people **135**.8–9
  and pollution **119**.12
  trends **119**.1
businesses and waste **111**.18
By Their Own Young Hand **136**.7

C

C8 event **110**.24
Cabinet, The **131**.21
caffeine **114**.5; **118**.35
  and mental health **141**.35

calcium **88**.6
  dietary sources **140**.4
  teenagers' requirements **123**.6–7
  and vegetarian diets **140**.3
call barring **134**.28
call centres **98**.19–20
calorie content of alcohol **143**.2
calorie intake **88**.1, 12
  recording **113**.31
calorie restriction, and life expectancy **105**.29, 32
camera phones and bullying **122**.22–3, 26
campaigns
  joining, and raising self-esteem **117**.33
  litter **111**.8, 12
  and the media **142**.10
  recycling **111**.25
  waste prevention **111**.16
campylobacter **88**.28
Canada, Beyond Compare Photo Tour **117**.13
cancer
  and alcohol consumption **60**.1, 15
  bladder cancer **60**.16, 17
  and blood cells **60**.34
  bone cancer **60**.9, 11, 35
  brain cancer **60**.5
  and cannabis use **128**.17, 19, 28
  causes of **60**.1, 8
  cells **60**.1, 33
  cervical cancer **60**.5, 14, 16
  childhood cancer **60**.8, 9–11, 13, 28, 32, 33–4
  colorectal (bowel) cancer **60**.3, 4, 6, 14, 16
  and complementary therapies **60**.39; **81**.3, 10, 21,
    27, 32–3
  and diet **60**.1–5, 14
  early detection of **60**.36
  and elderly people **60**.3, 7, 14
  environmental factors in **60**.1, 2
  and family history **60**.4, 5
  inequalities in cancer incidence and mortality **60**.14
  kidney cancer **60**.5, 9, 11, 16, 17
  leukaemia, stem cell therapy **144**.21
  liver cancer **60**.5, 9, 16, 17
  lung cancer **145**.34
  lymphomas **60**.4, 9, 10, 33
  melanoma (skin) cancer **60**.5, 18, 19–21
  metastases **60**.1, 8
  mouth, lips and throat cancer **60**.5, 15
  multiple myeloma **60**.5
  oesophageal cancer **60**.4, 15, 17
  and older people **105**.3
  ovarian cancer **60**.4, 11
  pancreatic cancer **60**.4, 16, 17
  and passive smoking **145**.2, 29
  prevention **60**.2, 3; **88**.17, 30
  prostate cancer **105**.10
  research **60**.2, 3
  research and animal experiments **103**.8, 10, 13
  and smoking **60**.1, 2, 3, 4, 13, 14, 15–17, 27; **145**.34
  stem cell therapy for blood cancers **144**.21
  stomach cancer **60**.4, 16, 17
  and sunlight **60**.1, 2

support for people living with **60**.38
survival rates **60**.4, 5, 13, 27
symptoms **60**.1–2
childhood cancers **60**.10, 11
testicular **60**.5, 11, 12, 13, 18, 26
thyroid cancer **60**.35
top ten cancer killers in the UK **60**.2
tumours **60**.1
and vegetarian diets **140**.9, 11
womb **60**.5
see also breast cancer; lung cancer; prostate cancer
cancer salves (escharotics) **81**.33
cancer treatments **60**.1, 4, 5
and age of patients **60**.7, 14
biopsies **60**.33–4
and body scanning **60**.35, 36–7
bone marrow transplants **60**.35, 36
chemotherapy **60**.1, 4, 5, 26, 33, 34, 35, 36
childhood cancer **60**.9, 33–4
and early diagnosis **60**.7
effectiveness of **60**.7
and genetically modified hens **138**.20–21
hormone therapy **60**.4, 35, 36
and hospices **60**.8, 13
laser treatment **60**.35
nuclear medicine or isotope scanning **60**.37
painkillers **60**.7–8
radiotherapy **60**.1, 4, 5, 25, 33, 34, 35, 36
surgery **60**.1, 4, 5, 26, 33–4, 35
cannabinoids **118**.38
and multiple sclerosis **128**.36
THC **128**.3, 34
cannabis **114**.38
appearance **128**.1
cannabis cafés 27–8
cannabis oil **128**.4, 6, 23
cannabis resin (hashish) **128**.1, 3, 6, 23
seizures of **128**.31
chemical content **128**.13–14
children's use **114**.20, 21; **128**.16
and depression **128**.14
classification **128**.13
compulsive use **128**.15
cultivation **128**.23–4; 33–4
penalties for **128**.31
skunk **128**.3–4
dealing, penalties for **128**.2, 9, 13
dependence on **128**.2, 8, 15
and driving **114**.23; **128**.14
eating **128**.5
and ecstasy **114**.16
effects of **114**.29
desired **128**.4, 14
harmful **128**.1–2, 4–5, 8–9, 13–15, 28
on the brain **128**.34
on learning and educational performance **128**.14
medicinal **128**.4, 28, 36, 37
skunk **128**.2
forms of **128**.1, 3–4, 6, 13
giving up **128**.2, 10
and hard drug use **128**.9–10, 11, 28

herbal cannabis (marijuana/grass) **128**.2,3,6, 23
seizures of **128**.31
history **128**.7
home cultivation of **128**.3–4, 30–31
and the law **114**.38; **128**.2, 7, 9, 26–38
legalisation debate **128**.7
market **128**.23–4
medicinal use of **114**.39; **128**.4, 28, 36, 37
and the law **128**.37
and multiple sclerosis **81**.30, 31; **128**.36, 37
and mental health **114**.37, 38; **128**.5, 8, 14–15
and multiple sclerosis **81**.30, 31; **128**.36, 37
names for **128**.1
penalties
for cultivation **128**.31
for possession **128**.2, 9, 13, 27, 30, 31, 32
for supply **128**.2, 9, 13
potency of **128**.6
resin **128**.3
skunk **128**.2
prices **128**.2, 6
production *see* cannabis cultivation
psychosis **128**.15
purity **128**.1, 2
reclassification of **114**.37; **128**.13, 26–8, 29
criticized **128**.38
effect on health **128**.30–32, 38
public attitudes to **128**.12
and respiratory health **128**.18–19
seizures of **128**.23, 31
smoking **128**.8
effects of **128**.5, 18–19
smuggling **114**.34
sources **128**.3, 34
THC (delta-9 tetrahydrocannabinol) **114**.37, 38;
128.3, 34
use
Europe **128**.21–2
giving up **128**.2, 10
methods of use **128**.5, 6, 13
prevalence **128**.6, 21, 22
public attitudes to **128**.12
users
children **114**.20, 21; **128**.16
cans, recycling **111**.11, 23, 26, 31
canvassers **131**.18
capital flows **98**.5, 18
capitalism **98**.2
carbohydrates **88**.2, 5–6, 15
carbon
carbon neutral societies/communities **95**.20, 29
low carbon technologies **97**.4
and permafrost **95**.15
reducing exhaust emissions **95**.27
and uncertainties about climate change **95**.7
carbon dioxide emissions **20**.23; **98**.14
and air transport **97**.25
and biomass **97**.18
and energy efficiency **95**.30, 32, 38
from fossil fuel burning **97**.1, 4
from power stations **97**.3

and global warming **95**.1, 2, 4, 5, 6, 9, 10
    levels in the atmosphere **95**.6, 10, 13, 19, 30
        and endangered species **95**.22
        and rivers **95**.21
    public awareness of **97**.34
    reducing **95**.3, 5, 8, 14; **97**.2
    from transport **119**.14, 15, 16, 24, 30
        in the UK **97**.5, 21
    see also greenhouse gas
carbon monoxide, transport emissions **119**.15
cardboard recycling **111**.27, 31, 36
cardio-respiratory endurance **113**.24
cardiology, stem cell therapy **144**.22, 23, 28
cardiovascular disease *see* heart disease
care gap **135**.20
care homes, older people in **105**.15
care leavers and homelessness **130**.11, 14
career advice **107**.32
    gender equality **112**.9, 21–2
career breaks **107**.27
career progression **107**.28
carers
    and flexible working **107**.17–18
    and people with mental health problems **105**.39
    young carers **135**.10–12
carotenes **88**.2, 5
cars
    attitudes to car use **97**.35, 36
        male **112**.30
    car clubs **119**.33
    cleaner fuels **119**.20–23
    congestion *see* congestion, traffic
    dependency on **119**.7
    drink-driving *see* drink-driving
    drugs and driving **114**.23–4
    and energy conservation **95**.5, 38
    fuel efficient **119**.20–24
    and greenhouse gases **95**.4
    ownership **119**.7, 11, 29
    recycling **111**.35
    reducing use of **119**.39
    sharing **119**.32–3
    speeding **119**.3, 4, 8
        and pedestrian injuries **119**.5, 30–31
        and speed cameras **119**.4, 17, 18
        speed limiters **119**.18
    spending on **134**.4, 25
    tax and fuel efficiency **119**.24
    usage trends **119**.1, 7–9, 11, 13, 29
    see also road accidents
cartilage repair using stem cells **144**.21
cartoons of Mohammed **121**.10–13, 15–16; **142**.34
cash use, regional differences, UK **110**.15
cashless society **74**.9–11
casinos **129**.2
    new, UK **129**.15, 34
    supercasino **129**.14–16, 34
catalogues and credit payment **134**.22
cathartic role of football **141**.32
Catholic Church
    and abortion **126**.2, 36

and assisted suicide **102**.15
    Catholic schools **94**.12–13, 30
    and contraception **20**.3; **126**.1–2
    tradition and beliefs **94**.2
    see also Christianity
cattle
    cloning **144**.36–8
    and hybrid embryos **144**.11
    see also livestock farming
CCTV (Closed Circuit Television) **82**.1, 6
    and crime prevention **82**.2, 3, 6
    and human rights **82**.24
    and RFID tags **82**.16
    statistics **82**.2
    and surveillance of public places **82**.3; **120**.33
    and workplace monitoring **82**.26, 27; **120**.32–3
celebrities
    influence on girls' body image **117**.20–21
    as parental role models **124**.6
    role models for boys **117**.23
cell culture **103**.14, 18, 19
cell nuclear replacement **144**.15
cemeteries **116**.37
censorship **121**.1–2
    films **121**.22, 23–5
    and the Internet **121**.18–21
    television **121**.36–7
census ethnic group questions **115**.3
Centrepoint
    debt advice **130**.25
    help for homeless young people **130**.22
cereals **88**.5–6, 15
cerebral palsy and learning disabilities **135**.34
cervical cancer **60**.5, 14, 16
CFCs (chlorofluorocarbons) **95**.1, 3, 4, 5
challenges as way of raising self-esteem **117**.33
challenging racism **115**.2
    at work **115**.12
charitable giving **130**.32, 33
charity foundation as remembrance **116**.17
chat rooms
    and bullying **122**.19–20, 21
    and online child abuse **104**.25
    and online safety **104**.20–1, 27, 35
    use by children and young people **104**.5, 20–1
Chechen conflict **92**.14, 16
    and child soldiers **99**.37
cheese and vegetarian diets **140**.6, 18, 22, 26
chemical/biological weapons, terrorist attacks using
    92.9, 31
chemicals recycling **111**.35
child abuse **120**.14–15; **132**.1–6
    abusers *see* child abusers
    care after abuse **132**.5
    definition **132**.1, 4
    and dependency **141**.10
    and dissociative disorders **141**.12–13
    effects of **132**.3, 4–5, 6, 22, 23
    emotional **132**.1, 5–6
        signs of **132**.4–5
    and false memory syndrome **132**.34–5

and low self-esteem **117**.7–8
and mental health problems **141**.10, 12–13
neglect **132**.1–2
  signs of **132**.4–5
online **104**.25; **132**.33
  images **132**.31–2
physical **132**.1
  signs of **132**.4
  see also corporal punishment; smacking
and the police **132**.3
and poverty **110**.39
signs of **132**.4–5
telling someone about the abuse **132**.23–4, 28
see also corporal punishment; sexual abuse; smacking
child abusers **132**.2, 4, 22
  children as **132**.29, 30
  help for **132**.36–9
  misconceptions about **132**.25
  see also paedophiles
child labour **99**.1–15; **110**.39; **120**.18–20
  and age of child **99**.2
  attitudes to **99**.1
  combating **99**.11–13
  defining **99**.2, 3
  demand for **99**.3
  domestic work **99**.1, 4, 7–10
  economic benefits of eliminating **99**.1, 6, 15
  economic truths of **99**.14–15
  and education **99**.3, 7, 10, 11–12, 15
  and human rights **99**.4, 6
  impact on a child **99**.2, 3
  legislation and laws
    enforcement of **99**.11
    improving **99**.11
  organisations to take action against **99**.4
  and poverty **99**.2, 3, 4, 11, 12, 14–15
  reasons for **99**.1, 2–3, 3–4
  statistics **99**.1, 2, 14
  suitability for certain types of work **99**.4
  and the tourist industry **109**.32
  types of **99**.1, 2, 3, 4
child participation, and children's rights **120**.9–11
child pornography **99**.1, 16, 17, 20, 24, 25
  online **132**.31–2
  viewed by young people **132**.30
child poverty
  global **110**.35, 36–7
  public awareness **110**.10
  statistics **110**.7, 12
  UK **110**.4, 5, 6–7, 10, 12, 13
Child Poverty Action Group **135**.6
Child Poverty in Rich Countries UNICEF report **110**.4
child prostitution **99**.1, 16, 17, 25–6, 27–8
child protection **120**.14–15; **132**.3, 5
  abuses **110**.39
child psychiatrists **100**.2
child safety concerns of parents **124**.13–14
Child Safety Orders **137**.12
child sex tourism **109**.32, 35–6
  awareness of **109**.36
  legal framework **109**.35–6

child soldiers **99**.1, 4, 29–39; **120**.20
  age of **99**.29–30
  benefits of ending child soldier use **99**.39
  defining **99**.29
  girls **99**.29, 31, 36
  harmful effects of being **99**.31, 36
  and human rights atrocities **99**.30
  and non-governmental armed groups **99**.30
  statistics **99**.29
  see also war-affected children
Child Support Agency **133**.34, 37
  problems **124**.35; **133**.30
Child Tax Credit (CTC) **110**.6, 7; **133**.33
childbirth
  deaths in **112**.39
  see also post-natal depression
childcare
  advice **133**.37–8
  careers, men **112**.23–4
  costs **124**.3
  emergency childcare **107**.22
  experience for teenagers **133**.27
  and fathers **124**.7–10, 11
  and flexible working **107**.12, 16, 21, 23
  and grandmothers **124**.37–8
  prohibition of physical punishment **132**.15
  underprovision **110**.6–7
childhood problems
  and dependency **141**.9–10
  and low self-esteem **117**.7–8, 31, 32–3
  and post traumatic stress disorder **141**.3
childhood obesity **88**.3, 11; **113**.1–5, 6, 7–8, 12; **127**.33, 36–7
  importance of exercise **113**.6
  measurement in schools **127**.36
  and television **113**.2
Childhood Under Threat, UNICEF report **110**.36
childless people **20**.26
childlessness for financial reasons **124**.18
ChildLine
  and bullying **122**.1, 2, 10, 12
  and child abuse **132**.2–3
  and eating disorders **127**.20–21
  and racism **115**.1
  and self-harm **123**.36–7
  and stepfamily worries **124**.23
  and suicide **123**.35
  and substance abuse **114**.27–8
childminders, prohibition of physical punishment **132**.15
children
  abuse *see* child abuse
  and advertising **134**.10, 12
  age and children's rights **120**.5
  alcohol consumption **143**.20
  alcohol and mental health problems **125**.9
  and bereavement **116**.1, 9, 19–28
  bereavement statistics **116**.20, 21
  bereavement support **116**.15, 28
  and body image **117**.14, 19, 22, 25
  cancer in childhood **60**.8, 9–11, 13, 28, 32, 33–4

as carers **135**.10–12
and censorship
    films **121**.23–5
    video games **121**.32–3
    videos **121**.26
childhood leukaemia and medical research **103**.12
of cohabiting couples **106**.21–2; **124**.22
and consumerism **134**.11–12
costs of raising **124**.3; **134**.25
and criminal justice **137**.11–12
cycling **119**.28, 30
death
    children's questions about **116**.26–7
    children's understanding of **116**.22
deaths of
    mortality rates **20**.36, 40
    and poverty **110**.35
and depression **123**.27–8; **125**.27–8
in developing countries
    deaths and diseases from water-related illness
    76.2, 3, 5, 9, 13, 14
    and global water supplies **76**.13–14
    and hygiene education **76**.14
    and sanitation provision **76**.13–14
    and water collection **76**.13, 19–20
developing responsibility **124**.13–14
diet **113**.4–5
disabled *see* disabled children
discipline *see* discipline
and divorce **106**.27, 33–8; **124**.24, 29–30, 32–4
and domestic violence
    blaming themselves **108**.20
    coping strategies **108**.23
    effects of **108**.11, 28
    and keeping women at home **108**.15
    living with abuse **108**.26, 27
    loss of confidence **108**.20
    and neglect **108**.20
    seeking professional help **108**.23, 28, 36
and drug use **114**.20–22, 25
of drug users **114**.28
drugs testing at school **114**.26
and eating disorders **127**.3, 20–21
ethnic minorities, and education **115**.18, 19–21
exercise, lack of **113**.1, 7, 8
falling out with parents **124**.18
and fathers **124**.7–11
and food advertising **88**.10, 11, 20, 35, 37
and food in school **123**.32
and funerals **116**.23, 26
and gambling
    online gambling **129**.18
    protection by Gambling Commission **129**.4
    Scotland **129**.32–3
gender development **112**.35
and grief **116**.19–28
health, and transport **119**.13–14, 31
and HIV/AIDS **96**.20, 39
and homelessness **130**.23
inactivity **113**.1, 7, 8
and the Internet **104**.3–5, 9–11, 13, 17–29

of lone parents **124**.33–4; **133**.28, 31
and male carers **112**.23
and media violence **121**.33, 34, 35
and mental health
    mental health problems **125**.16; **141**.1, 20–21
    mental health programmes **141**.37
    effect of parents' mental health problems
        141.24–5
and mobile phone tracking **82**.19, 20
and money matters **74**.6–7, 12–13
needs **120**.2
naming after brands **134**.12
obesity *see* childhood obesity
and passive smoking **60**.17; **145**.2, 28–9
and poverty *see* child poverty
and prison *see* youth custody
and racism **115**.1–2, 9
refugees **89**.39; **120**.21–2
and road accidents **119**.5, 28, 30–31
and road safety **119**.5–6
safety concerns of parents **124**.13–14; **137**.20
sex education **133**.15, 17
sexual abuse *see* sexual abuse
smacking *see* smacking
and smoking **123**.11–13; **145**.2–3
    attitudes to smoking **145**.20
    health effects **145**.2
    and the law **145**.3
    mother smoking in pregnancy **145**.32–3
    effects of nicotine **145**.27
    passive smoking **145**.2, 28–9
and sport safety **113**.28
and stepfamilies **124**.23–8
and suicide **123**.35
and sun exposure **60**.19, 20–1
of teenage mothers **133**.10
and television
    parental control of viewing **121**.26, 27, 34
time spent with parents **106**.2
    fathers **124**.7–8, 9, 11
travel to school **119**.26, 29–30
as victims **110**.39
and video classification **121**.32–3
and video games **121**.32–3
wealth **110**.10
see also boys and young men; girls and young women;
    young people
Children's Act
    and child protection **120**.15
    and physical punishment **132**.8
Children's Commissioner, views on bullying **122**.7, 17
children's rights **120**.1–22
    African Movement **120**.19–20
    and age of children **120**.1, 2
    and child abuse **120**.14–15
    and children's needs **120**.2
    Committee on the Rights of the Child **120**.4
    and justice system **120**.1–2, 12–13
    and participation in decision-making **120**.9–11
    denied by poverty **110**.36–7
    refugees **120**.21–2

and responsibilities **120**.1
    timeline **120**.3
    to vote **120**.7–8
    in the UK **120**.2
    UN Convention on the Rights of the Child **120**.4–6
Children's Rights Alliance for England (CRAE)
    120.7, 17
chimeras **144**.10–12
China
    cigarette manufacture and consumption **145**.22
    Internet censorship **121**.2, 19, 20–21
Chinese football players **118**.13
Chinese medicine **81**.2, 3
    and cancer **81**.33
    and endangered species **81**.15
    herbal medicine **81**.14–15, 39
    see also complementary medicine (CM)
chiropractic **81**.8–9, 23, 36
    effectiveness of **81**.24
    misdiagnosis and dangers of **81**.23, 24
    regulation of **81**.23
    and scientists **81**.28, 29
chlamydia **96**.2–3, 4, 9; **123**.26
    and HIV **96**.12
    increase in cases of **96**.8, 10
    signs and symptoms **96**.5
    testing for **96**.2, 3, 5
    treatment **96**.5
chocolate **88**.18–19, 31
    vegan **140**.22, 26
choice as consumer right **134**.1
cholera **76**.2, 12, 13, 32
cholesterol and exercise **113**.34
Choose Life, suicide prevention strategy **136**.34
CHP (Combined Heat and Power) plants **97**.2, 4
Christianity
    and abortion and contraception **126**.1–2
    beliefs **94**.1–2, 3
    and the Census (2001) **94**.3, 5, 6, 28
    and church attendance **94**.5, 6
    and faith **94**.39
    festivals **94**.3
    funerals **116**.33
    Golden Rule **94**.8, 11
    and homosexuality **101**.5–7
    and 'honour killings' **94**.30
    new religious movements/cults **94**.19, 21, 25
    and RE (religious education) **94**.9, 15
    and young people **94**.6–7
Christmas waste **111**.5
church attendance, effect on young people **137**.26
Church of England **94**.1, 3
    and abortion and contraception **126**.1
    disestablishment **94**.37
    and marriage **106**.9–10
    and RE (religious education) **94**.15, 31
    schools **94**.12–14, 30
Church of Scotland and ethics of human cloning
    144.5–6
cider, strength of **143**.1
cigarettes **114**.5

chemicals in **145**.1
    cost **145**.3, 17
    pack size **145**.19
    sales, effect of smoking ban **145**.16–17
    see also smoking
Circles of Support, for sex offenders **132**.37–9
cities *see* cars, congestion; urban areas; urban growth
citizen photojournalism **142**.23
Citizens Advice Bureaux, debt advice **134**.23
citizenship **89**.37
    British identity **131**.1–14
    European Union **131**.38
    global **131**.37
    government **131**.15–25
    survey **131**.2–3
    test **131**.12
    young people **131**.26–39
Citizenship Education in schools **108**.25; **131**.36
city colleges and special educational needs **135**.36
civic involvement, young people **131**.31–2
civil law **137**.1
civil liberties
    and drugs legalisation **114**.39
    and media regulation **142**.1–2
Civil Partnerships **101**.9, 10, 23, 29, 32, 33–5
civil protest **121**.14
civil service, women in **112**.18
civil wars **89**.7–8
CJD (Creutzfeld Jacob disease) **141**.7
clandestine marriages **106**.9–10
Clarence Court eggs **140**.39
class *see* social class
class A drugs
    prices **114**.6–7
    use increasing **114**.14
    young people's use **114**.21
class sizes (schools) **139**.1, 12
classification
    of drugs **114**.1, 31, 32; **128**.26
    of films **121**.22, 23–5, 29–30
    of video games **121**.32–3
classrooms and gender equality **112**.10
Clean Up Television Campaign **121**.36
cleaner fuels **119**.20–23
Cleaner Neighbourhoods and Environment Act
    111.19, 21
Clearfield CL131 rice **138**.20
clearing (university entrance) **139**.30
clenbuterol hydrochloride **118**.35
climate change
    abrupt **95**.17–20
    and consumerism **134**.31
    dangerous **95**.12
    deaths attributed to **95**.11, 23, 25, 38, 39
    economic costs of **95**.25
    effects of **95**.11–28
    and food production **140**.17, 37
    and global water supplies **76**.1, 3, 5, 8
    information on **95**.1–10
    and meat production **140**.17
    misconceptions **95**.3

and nuclear power **97**.19–20, 21, 22
and oil production **95**.16–17
positive and negative feedbacks **95**.8, 10, 15
public awareness of factors contributing to **97**.34
reasons for **95**.2, 9
and renewable energy sources
bioenergy **97**.18
case for **97**.1–2
and wind energy **97**.15
and social justice **95**.16, 17
solutions **95**.29–39
and species extinction **78**.10, 11
and transport emissions **119**.14, 30
in the UK **95**.3, 5, 15, 17
and water management **76**.34
see also energy efficiency; global warming;
greenhouse
gas emissions
cloning
animals **144**.30–39
definition **144**.1, 4, 5, 18
ethical issues **144**.2–3, 5–6, 7–8
and factory farming **144**.35
and food production **144**.36–9
how it works **144**.1, 4, 14
human **144**.1–14
natural **144**.1
regulations **144**.3
risks **144**.2, 3, 6, 8
Clubs for Young People (CYP) **118**.2
co-education, effect on girls **112**.6
co-parenting after divorce **124**.32
coaches, sports
female **118**.20
and pressure to use drugs **118**.29
coal, as an energy source **97**.4
coastal areas
development and population growth **20**.14, 22, 24
flooding and climate change **95**.2, 3, 5, 7, 9, 11, 14,
15
cocaine **114**.5, 10
mixed with other drugs **114**.16
prevalence of use **114**.14
prices **114**.7
smuggling **114**.34
see also crack cocaine
cocoa industry and child labour **120**.19
coffee growers **98**.13, 17
poverty due to trade rules **110**.22
Cognitive Behavioural Therapy (CBT) **141**.35
and bipolar disorder **141**.14–15
for bulimia nervosa (CBT-BN) **127**.14
and giving up cannabis use **128**.10
and self-harm **136**.11
and Seasonal Affective Disorder **125**.38
cohabitation
age at first **106**.10
changing views on **106**.4
and stability for children **124**.22
and 'common law' marriages **106**.8
legal protection for cohabitees **106**.7–8, 10

and likelihood of marriage **106**.5
reasons for **106**.11
and splitting up **106**.21
statistics **20**.26
collagen, stem cell therapy **144**.21–2
colorectal (bowel) cancer **60**.3, 4, 6, 14, 16
colour as grounds for discrimination **115**.7
Columbus eggs **140**.39
commercialization
effect on children **134**.11–12
in sport **118**.9
Committed 2 Equality (C2E) **115**.13
Committee of Advertising Practice (CAP) **134**.10
commodity prices **98**.10, 17
'common law' marriages **106**.8, 9–10
communication
and abortion **126**.11
importance in bereavement **116**.24–5
importance in depression **125**.3, 39
young people **125**.8
and eating disorders **127**.30
and self-esteem **117**.4
Communications Act and media mergers **142**.4
communications data **82**.5, 33–4
government monitoring of **82**.1–2
and the law **82**.33–4
communities
and identity cards **82**.11
sustainable **85**.32, 38, 39
community arts **141**.38
community cohesion **131**.2
community involvement, young people **131**.32
community sentences **137**.12
community stewardship of natural resources **110**.26
community-based tourism **109**.19, 27, 33–4, 38
company directors, female **112**.18
compassion, and euthanasia **102**.12–13, 30
compensation for faulty goods **134**.2, 17
competition and consumer choice **134**.1
competition scams **134**.26
competitive sport in schools **118**.4
complaints
about goods **134**.2, 17
sex discrimination **112**.14
complementary medicine (CM)
and cancer **60**.39
and consumer choice **81**.37
and consumer ignorance **81**.35
defining **81**.1, 4
and depression **125**.39
manic depression **125**.20
and diagnosis **81**.34
disciplines within **81**.1–3
effectiveness of **81**.22–4, 26, 27, 31
expenditure on **81**.23, 37, 39
and GPs **81**.21
impact on wildlife **78**.23
and misdiagnosis **81**.23
and multiple sclerosis **81**.30–1
and the placebo effect **81**.26, 28, 34
regulation of **81**.23

safety of **81**.27, 31
  and scientists **81**.28–9
  and self-care **81**.36–7
  why bogus therapies seem to work **81**.34
  see also Chinese medicine
complex carbohydrates **88**.2
compost **111**.3
composting waste **111**.6, 23, 31, 33
compulsions (obsessional rituals) **141**.17
compulsive eating **127**.20–21
compulsive exercise **113**.37–8
compulsive gambling **129**.2, 27–39
  causes **129**.29
  definition **129**.11
  drug treatment **129**.39
  and Gambling Commission **129**.5
  help for **129**.5, 29, 36, 37, 39
  online gambling **129**.21–2
  signs **129**.28, 29, 35–6, 38
  support groups **129**.37
  under 16s **129**.13, 25, 32–3
  women **129**.34
compulsive shopping **134**.13, 14
compulsory admission for eating disorders **127**.29
compulsory turnout to vote **131**.20–21
computer games
  and boys' underachievement **112**.3
  violence, influence on children **121**.32–3, 35
computer research, in medicine **103**.13–14, 17, 19, 22
computers
  and academic achievement **112**.3
  home computer ownership **134**.5
  and older people **105**.5
  see also Internet
conception **123**.22; **133**.8
  rate, young people **126**.30–31; **133**.2
condoms **101**.3–4; **123**.23
  availability of **96**.2
  and HIV **96**.12, 14, 16, 24, 25, 29, 30, 32, 33, 34
  and the prevention of STIs **96**.1–2, 9; **123**.24, 25
confidence
  self-confidence *see* self-esteem
confidentiality
  and abortion **126**.13, 28, 29
    effect on teenage conception rate **126**.30
  and eating disorders **127**.28
Confucianism **94**.11
congestion, traffic **119**.11
  congestion charging **119**.12, 34–5, 38
  rail **119**.35
  and road building **119**.12
conservation
  animal species **78**.11
  and the exotic pet trade **78**.21–2
  plant species **78**.17
  tree species **78**.12
  zoo conservation **78**.24–5
  see also endangered species; extinction
Conservative party
  and GM crops **138**.39
  policies on crime **137**.2

conspicuous compassion **116**.17–18
constitutional change, impact on national identity **131**.5, 6
construction industry, recruitment of women **112**.25
consumer assurance **134**.33–4
consumer choice **134**.1
consumer credit debt **134**.4, 23
Consumer Direct advice line **134**.21
consumer durables **134**.3–4, 5
consumer organisations **134**.21
consumer rights **134**.1–2, 17–21
  faulty goods **134**.2, 17
  and guarantees **134**.18–19
  private sales and auctions **134**.20
  and safety **134**.2
  secondhand goods **134**.20
consumer spending **134**.3–4
  see also shopping
consumer terrorism **92**.11
Consumer Voice **134**.21
consumerism
  and mental health problems **134**.5
  and relative poverty **110**.22–3
consumers **134**.1
  and animal welfare **140**.31, 33
  and child labour **99**.12
  ethical behaviour **134**.33–5
  and genetic modification **138**.9
  and RFID tags **82**.16–17, 35
  rights *see* consumer rights
  satisfaction **134**.6
  spending *see* consumer spending
consumption
  and population growth **20**.8, 22–3, 24
Contact and Assessment Teams **130**.31
contained (indoor) GMOs **138**.12
content sharing sites **142**.35
contraception **123**.22–3
  advice **126**.23–4
  'double dutch' method of **96**.2
  emergency contraception (EC) **126**.24
  and the male pill **20**.38–9
  and men **96**.13
  and microbicides **96**.34
  and population growth **20**.3
  religious views **126**.1–3
  and young people **123**.22–3; **133**.1, 2, 17
  see also condoms; family planning; pill, contraceptive
contract sales **107**.22
contributory benefits **110**.18
controlling behaviour **108**.2, 15, 19
Convention on the Rights of the Child, and corporal punishment **132**.17
Cooperative Bank Ethical Consumerism Report **134**.32
Copenhagen Declaration on Anti-Doping in Sport **118**.27
copycat behaviour, self-harm **136**.10
copyright and Freedom of Information Act **142**.19
coral reefs, and climate change **95**.11, 13
coral trade **78**.21
coronary heart disease (CHD) *see* heart disease

coroner **116**.32
corporal punishment **132**.7–21
  abolishing **132**.13
  and children's rights **120**.15
  effects of **132**.9–10, 13
  and human rights **132**.9, 12–13, 16–17
  ineffectiveness **132**.9
  legal position **132**.15
  prevalence of **132**.15–16
  in schools, globally **132**.7
  as stress relief for adults **132**.10
corporate accountability **98**.27
corporate globalisation **98**.25–7
corporate lobbying **98**.4
corporate responsibility **98**.6, 26, 29, 37–8
cosmetic testing on animals **103**.23
cosmetic surgery **117**.21, 24–5
  and ethnicity **117**.29–30
  and stem cell therapy **144**.24–5
costs
  of abortion **126**.12
  academies **139**.15
  of alcohol, effect on consumption **143**.17, 31
  of alcohol misuse **143**.36
  of the asylum system **89**.11, 30
  of cannabis **128**.2, 6
  of cleaner vehicles **119**.20–24
  of coronary heart disease **113**.20
  of crime **137**.2
  of disability **135**.5, 17, 18
  of domestic violence **108**.10
  of education **139**.1, 35
    developing countries **110**.38
  of gym membership **113**.36
  of identity cards **120**.35–6; **131**.13
  of imprisonment **137**.37
  of litter clearing **111**.8
  of mental health problems **125**.16
  of motoring **119**.14
  of obesity **127**.33–4, 37
  of poverty elimination **110**.23
  of psychological therapy **125**.7
  of raising a child **124**.3
    as reason for smaller families **124**.18
  of smoking **145**.3, 17, 38
  of solicitors **137**.36
  university degrees **139**.35
  of vegan diet **140**.25
  of waste **111**.18
cotinine **145**.26
cotton **98**.24
  genetically modified **138**.35
council tax
  benefit **135**.5
  lone parents **133**.35, 38
  and pensioners **110**.19
counselling **141**.35
  for alcohol abuse **143**.25, 38
  for childhood bullying **122**.6
  for depression **125**.30–31
  eating disorders **127**.21, 29

  and help with stress **100**.32, 34
  for post–natal depression **125**.18
  for sexual abuse **132**.24
  and testing for HIV **96**.1
  and voluntary euthanasia **102**.2
counter-terrorism **92**.13
  aviation security **92**.32, 34
  contingency planning and resilience **92**.33
  counter-terrorist measures in London **92**.31–2
  and Islam **92**.26, 28–9
  public attitudes to **92**.35
  security measures **92**.38
  targeting terrorist funds **92**.22
  White convictions in the UK **92**.27–8
country of birth *see* birth country
countryside, and the production and use of energy
  97.24–5
Countryside Live **117**.38
county courts **137**.36
courts of law
  children's access to **120**.1–2
  court hearings **137**.36
  and debts **74**.35
  and torture evidence **120**.39
cows *see* cattle
crack cocaine **114**.10
  increasing usage **114**.14
  prices **114**.7
  see also cocaine
cranial osteopathy **81**.2
creativity
  and help for self-harm **136**.3
  and mental health **141**.38
credit
  advantages and disadvantages of **74**.23
  bank overdrafts **74**.1, 18, 19, 21–2
  consumer credit levels **134**.4, 23, 24
  credit ratings **74**.25, 27
  and homeless young people **130**.25–6
  interest rates **74**.23
  obtaining **74**.23
  and students **74**.30
  types of **134**.22
  using wisely **134**.22
  see also debt
credit cards **74**.26–7; **134**.22, 24
  and the cashless society **74**.9–11
  and consumer rights **134**.18
  credit reference agencies **74**.25, 27
  and e-shopping **104**.5, 6
  interest rates **74**.26, 27
  limits **74**.26
  minimum repayments **74**.26
  'payment holidays' **74**.26
  shopping around for **74**.25–6
  store cards **74**.27
  and students **74**.3, 30, 32, 36, 37
  theft, and RFID tags **82**.16
  and young people **74**.15, 16, 23
cremation **116**.37–8

crime
  costs of **137.2**
  definition **137.1**, 3
  detection rates **137.3–4**
  and divorce **106.31**
  and drug users **114.12**
  Europe **137.6**
  fear of **137.5**, 7
  hate crime **101.29**, 36–7
  and identity cards
    forging **82.7**, 8
    as a means of combating crime **82.7**, 8, 10, 11
  and licensing hours change **143.23**
  and the media **137.2**
  non-reporting, reasons for **137.31**
  public worry about **137.5**, 7
  racially motivated **115.9–10**
  religiously motivated **115.27**
  reporting **137.28**, 30–31
  and RFID cards **82.17**
  statistics **137.3–4**
  and surveillance **82.17–18**
  terrorism and organised crime **92.22**
  trends **137.1**, 4
  victims of *see* victims of crime
  victim personal statement **137.31**
  waste dumping **111.20**
  wildlife **78.19**, 38–9
  see also fraud; victims of crime; violent crime; young
    offenders
crime prevention
  and CCTV **82.2**, 3, 6
  and the Internet
    child protection **104.28–9**
    pharming **104.33–4**
    phishing **104.32–3**
Crimestoppers **137.31**
criminal injuries compensation **137.28**
criminal justice bill **137.29–30**
Criminal Justice and Public Order Act 1994 **121.31**
criminal justice system
  and children's rights **120.12**
  costs of domestic violence to **108.10**
  and young offenders **137.12**, 17
criminal offences **137.1**
criminal responsibility, age of **137.11**, 13
criminality
  and high self-esteem **117.7**
  and mental health problems **125.16**
crisis services, manic depression **125.20**
criticism **117.2–3**
crocodile farming **140.30**
crop biotechnology *see* genetically modified (GM) crops
crop rotation **88.14**
cross-contamination, genetic **138.4**
cross-cultural communication **142.34**
cross-pollination, GM and non-GM crops **138.6–7**,
    12–13
cross training **113.28**
Crown Court **137.36**
crystal healing **81.2**

CSA problems, single parent families **124.35**
cults *see* NRMs (New Religious Movements)
cultural differences and mixed-faith relationships
    115.39
cultural traditions
  British **131.1**
  and children's rights **120.2**
culture
  and corporal punishment **132.10**
  and religion **126.1**
  and the media **142.34**
curfew orders **137.12**
currency speculation **98.38**
current account balances, regional differences **110.15**
curriculum, schools, gender equality **112.9**
Cushing's syndrome and depression **125.5**
custody *see* prison; youth custody
customer service satisfaction **134.6**
cuts, first aid **136.22–3**
cutting (self-harm), safety measures **136.22**
cyanovirin-N **138.22**
cyber-bullying **122.19–26**
cybrids (animal-human hybrids) **144.9**, 10–12
cycle of abuse **132.25**
cycling **119.25**, 29
  children **119.28**; **124.14**
  health benefits **119.39**
  helmets **119.28**
  to school **119.30**
cystic fibrosis research, animal experimentation **144.34**

D

D notice **121.37**
D&E (surgical dilation and evacuation) **126.10**, 14
daily benchmarks for alcohol consumption **143.8**, 25,
    26–7, 34
  awareness of **143.11**, 34
dairy foods **88.6**, 15
dairy-free diet **140.22–3**, 26
data protection
  communications data **82.33–4**
  and RFID tags **82.16**
  and self-regulation **82.5**
Data Protection Acts **82.21–2**, 37–8, 39
day centres for homeless people **130.31**
daylight, effect on mental health **141.35**
DBD (disruptive behaviour disorder) influence of
    media violence **121.35**
DDNOS (dissociative disorder not otherwise specified)
    141.12
deaths **20.25**, 27, 30
  abortion-related **20.25**, 27, 30
  AIDS, impact on children **110.37**
  alcohol-related **143.3**, 6, 37
  cancer **60.3**, 7, 27; **81.23**, 32
    and hospices **60.8**
    lung cancer **60.3**, 15, 27
    skin cancer **60.19**
    and smoking **60.15**, 27

of children
    cyclists **119**.28
    mortality rates **20**.36, 40
    pedestrians **119**.5, 30
    and poverty **110**.35
children's questions about death **116**.26–7
children's understanding of death **116**.22
and cohabitation **106**.8
and drug misuse **114**.12, 13
ex-prisoners **114**.14
excess winter mortality **105**.5; 110.19
formal procedures **116**.29–32
from heart disease **113**.19
in hospital **116**.31
infant mortality **20**.28, 29, 30, 31; 105.2
maternal mortality **20**.25, 28, 29, 30, 36, 37, 39
older people, winter **110**.19
registering **116**.31
in road accidents **119**.4, 5, 30
from smoking **145**.1, 4, 12, 22, 24
unexpected **116**.31
from water-related diseases **76**.2, 9, 13, 14, 20, 35
debit cards **134**.24
    and the cashless society **74**.9–11
    and young people **74**.23–4
debt **134**.23–5
    advice **134**.23, 25
    attitudes to **74**.5
    buying on credit **134**.22
    calculating total repayments **74**.26
    communication with creditors **74**.25
    and families **74**.3, 5–6
    getting out of **74**.16
    and homeless young people **130**.24–6
    managing **74**.34–5
    regional differences, UK **110**.15
    repayments **98**.3, 7–8, 31, 38, 39
    statistics **134**.4, 23, 24
    students **74**.3, 5, 19–20, 31–2, 34–9; **134**.24
        amounts of debt **74**.36
        calculating essential expenditure **74**.34
        coping with **74**.28–9, 34–5
        court and summonses **74**.35
        and credit cards **74**.3, 30, 32, 36, 37
        maximising your income **74**.34
        overdrafts **74**.1, 21–2
        priority debts **74**.34–5
    tips for cutting **74**.25–6
    and unauthorised money lenders **74**.24
    world debt **110**.27–8
        public opinions **110**.34
    and young people **74**.1, 2, 15, 16, 23; **134**.24
decision-making
    children's participation in **120**.9–11
    and self-esteem **117**.37
    young people **131**.28
        feelings of exclusion **131**.26
decontamination of land, by plants **138**.14
decriminalization of cannabis **128**.7, 12
deer
    as food **140**.15, 17

hunting **103**.24, 28, 29
defensive eating **113**.32
deforestation **78**.11, 18; **95**.4, 5, 13, 15
    and global warming **95**.4, 5, 13, 15
    and population growth **20**.1, 14, 23, 24
    and water shortages **76**.21, 36
degrees, university
    costs **139**.34, 35
    courses **139**.2, 29, 30, 38–9
    and earnings **139**.35, 36, 37
    and ethnicity **139**.8
    and gender **112**.1, 8; **139**.10
    results rising **139**.33
Deliberate Release Directive **138**.4
delinquency, effect of divorce **124**.34
dementia **141**.6–8
    and advance directives **102**.33, 36
    and capacity **105**.39
    causes and prevention **105**.37
    and depression **105**.38; **125**.5
    and people in care homes **105**.15
    preventing **105**.30
    statistics **105**.3, 5, 37; **125**.16
    see also Alzheimer's disease
democracy
    and extremism **131**.23–4
    proposal for reform **131**.25
    see also elections
Denmark, cartoons of Mohammed **121**.10–13, 15–16;
    142.34
dental dams **96**.2; **101**.4
dependency **141**.9–10
depersonalisation **141**.11
deportation as anti-terrorism measure **120**.38–9
depressant drugs **114**.1, 5, 29
    alcohol **143**.4
depression **125**.1–23
    and abortion **126**.11
    and alcohol **125**.2, 3, 36–7; **143**.4
    anti-depressant drugs *see* anti-depressant drugs
    and assisted suicide **102**.6, 7, 30, 31
    and cannabis use **128**.14
    causes of **125**.2, 6, 19, 23
    in children and young people **123**.27–8; **125**.8,
        9, 27–8
    and complementary therapies **81**.30, 31; **125**.20, 39
    endogenous **125**.4
    and exam stress **100**.7
    and exercise **141**.39
    genetic factors in **125**.2
    and grief **116**.5, 19
    and incapacity benefit **100**.23
    manic depression *see* bipolar affective disorder
    and men **125**.13–15
    and obesity **113**.10
    in older people **105**.38, 39; **125**.22–3
    and personality **125**.2
    and physical activity **113**.29–30; **125**.3, 20, 39
    and physical illness **125**.2, 5–6
    post-natal **125**.4, 17–18
prevalence of **141**.1, 2

reactive **125**.4
seeking help **125**.2–3
and sexual abuse **132**.28
statistics on **136**.33
and stress **100**.1, 24
and suicide **125**.10
symptoms of **125**.1, 13
    in the elderly **125**.22–3
    manic depression **125**.19
    post-natal depression **125**.17
    seasonal affective disorder **125**.18
teenagers **125**.8
treatment of **125**.24–39
    children and young people **125**.8, 27–8
    diet **125**.3, 39
    drugs **125**.7, 19, 22, 24–5, 32, 35
    ECT (electroconvulsive therapy) **125**.25–6, 34, 35
    elderly people **125**.23
    manic depression **125**.19–20
    post-natal depression **125**.17–18
    psychotherapies **125**.29–31
    Seasonal Affective Disorder **125**.18
    self-help **125**.3, 39
    talking therapies **125**.29–31
types of **125**.4
and underage drinking **125**.9
unipolar (endogenous) **125**.4, 10
see also bipolar affective disorder, (manic depression);
    seasonal affective disorder (SAD)
derealisation **141**.11
desertification, and water shortages **76**.21, 36
detention
    of children **120**.12; 17
    of refugee children **120**.21
detention centres **89**.12, 13
    restraint techniques **120**.17
detoxification **143**.38
developing countries
    ageing population **20**.9, 11
    aid to **110**.28, 34
    AIDS/HIV in **96**.17–18, 36–7
    alcohol consumption **143**.6
    child labour in **99**.1, 2
    and climate change **95**.12–13, 14
    and disability **135**.25, 26–7
    education in **20**.20, 28
        prohibitive cost **110**.38
        and urban growth **20**.18
        women and girls **20**.3, 9, 18
    effect of EU GM controls **138**.29–30
    and GM crops **138**.9, 10, 23, 34–5
    life expectancy **20**.5
    population growth **20**.1–2, 4, 5, 8–9, 10
    and the right to water **76**.24–5, 32
    shantytowns **20**.17–18, 20
    and smoking **145**.22–4
    and tourism **109**.32–3
        pro-poor **109**.27, 38
        responsible **109**.18–20, 30
        working conditions in the tourist industry **109**.30,
            31, 32

urban growth **20**.9, 11, 17–20, 33
water collection **76**.13, 19–20
water pollution **76**.4, 10
water and sanitation services **76**.7, 8, 12, 17, 21
water shortages **76**.16, 19, 21
    and agriculture **76**.3, 4
    and aid programmes **76**.5
    statistics **76**.2, 6, 7
young people **20**.10–11, 33–4, 40
devolution, effect on national identity **131**.5, 6
diabetes
    and complementary therapies **81**.21
    and exercise **113**.34
    and obesity **113**.15; **127**.34
diarrhoea
    and access to safe water and sanitation **76**.17
    deaths from **76**.14, 30
    and hygiene promotion **76**.6, 12
    links to contaminated water **76**.5, 12
diary-keeping as way of remembrance **116**.16
diet
    and cancer **60**.1–5, 14
    and cancer treatments **81**.32–3
    and child behaviour **120**.16
    and children **113**.4–5, 8
    and coronary heart disease **113**.20
    and depression **125**.3, 39
    dietary trends **125**.11–12
    fat in the diet **113**.14, 20
    healthy *see* healthy eating
    and life expectancy **105**.1–2, 9, 10
    and mental health **125**.11–12; **141**.30–31, 34
    and Seasonal Affective Disorder **125**.38
    and stress **100**.19, 30, 31, 35
    teenage girls **117**.20, 21
    and weight maintenance **113**.31–2
    young people **123**.1, 6–7; **31**
    see also eating disorders; food and nutrition; healthy
        eating; veganism; vegetarianism
dietary obsession (orthorexia nervosa) **127**.19
dieting **113**.33
    girls and young women **117**.20–21
dignity *see* human dignity
dinosaurs
    extinction of **78**.1
    and global warming **95**.5, 9
direct debit **74**.9, 19, 24
direct mail scams **134**.26–8
direct racial discrimination **115**.7, 11
direct sex discrimination **112**.13
directorships, women **112**.18
disability
    benefits **135**.3, 4, 5–6
    and child poverty **110**.13
    costs of **135**.5, 17, 18
    definition **135**.2
    discrimination **135**.1, 3, 28–9
        workplace **135**.15
        see also Disability Discrimination Act
    and employment **107**.12; **135**.3, 4, 14, 15
    and the media **135**.29, 32, 35

and poverty **135**.16, 17–18
public attitudes to **135**.1, 30–31
UK statistics **135**.1, 2–3, 6
worldwide statistics **135**.25
Disability Agenda, DRC **135**.16, 31
Disability Discrimination Act **135**.13, 22, 31
and schools **135**.38–9
and workplace stress **100**.17, 20, 22
Disability Employment Advisers **135**.4
Disability Equality Duty **135**.13
and schools **135**.38–9
Disability Living Allowance **135**.5
disability rights, UN treaty **135**.26
Disability Rights Commission **135**.16, 31
Independence Day report **135**.20
Disability Rights Handbook **135**.6
disability symbol **135**.14
disabled babies
and abortion **126**.9, 34, 35
killing of newborn **102**.25
disabled children **107**.21
choice in education **135**.24–5
in developing countries **135**.26
resources for **135**.21
and sexual development **132**.29
violence against **135**.27
disabled people
discrimination **135**.1, 3
see also Disability discrimination Act
and employment **107**.12; **135**.3, 4, 14, 15
and football **118**.22
and the law on euthanasia **102**.11
and transport **135**.7–9
see also disability; learning disabilities
disabled person's railcard **135**.8
Disabled Person's Tax Credit **135**.5
disablism **135**.28–9
see also discrimination, disabled people
discipline
approaches to **132**.18
parental **124**.2
in schools
and gender equality **112**.10
problems **120**.16
see also corporal punishment; smacking
discomfort after exercise **113**.27
discrimination
and child labour **99**.4
direct and indirect **115**.7, 11
disabled people **135**.1, 3, 15, 28–9
see also Disability Discrimination Act **135**.13, 22,
31, 38–9
racial *see* racial discrimination
refugee children **120**.22
in the workplace **101**.23–4, 29, 35–6; **135**.15
see also ageism; prejudice; racism; religious
discrimination; sex discrimination
disease
age-related diseases **105**.3, 32
and medical research **103**.12–13, 16
and population growth **20**.6, 19, 20

of poverty and wealth **110**.35
water-related **76**.2, 3, 5, 6, 9, 12, 19, 20, 35
and children **76**.2, 3, 5, 9, 13
displaced persons **89**.1, 6, 8–9
disposable nappies, environmental impact **111**.13–15
disruptive behaviour disorder, influence of media
violence **121**.35
dissociative disorders **141**.11–13
distraction techniques, self-harmers **136**.5, 16, 19, 21
diuretics **118**.35, 37
diversity
as business benefit **135**.14
and sport **118**.12
divorce **106**.27–39
and children **124**.29–30, 32, 33–4
and male depression **125**.14
reaction to, gender differences **112**.32
DIY abortions **126**.32–4
DIY burials **116**.38–9
DNA **138**.4, 12; **144**.17
Do Somethin' campaign **118**.2
doctors
and abortion **126**.12, 13, 24
and bereavement support **116**.2
and cancer **60**.6, 7, 32, 38
cancer specialists (oncologists) **60**.14, 31, 36
and complementary medicine **60**.39; **81**.4
consultants **60**.31
and disability support **135**.4
and euthanasia **102**.2, 4, 13, 14, 31
fears of rise in gambling **129**.31
and help for eating disorders **127**.28
and medically assisted dying in the UK **102**.20–1
and reporting a death **116**.31
see also GPs (general practitioners); physician-
assisted suicide (PAS)
Dolly the sheep **144**.1, 15, 30–31, 32, 34, 39
domestic appliances, household ownership **134**.3–4, 5
Domestic Testing Pool (DTP) **118**.31
domestic violence **108**.1–18; **112**.39; **124**.18; **137**.8
changing abusers behaviour **108**.11–12, 33
in childhood, and low self-esteem **117**.32
cycle of abuse **108**.1, 11–12
definition **108**.1, 19, 24, 28
extent and facts about **108**.4, 7–8, 9–10, 19
helplines **108**.3, 14, 20, 21, 31, 37; **133**.37
and housing support **130**.30
injuries sustained **108**.9, 10
leaving home **108**.7–8, 9–10, 12, 21, 37
refuges **108**.32–33
legal protection **108**.38–9
living with abuse **108**.11, 15–16, 18
long-term effects **108**.1–2
and low self-esteem **108**.1, 2; **117**.32
male victims **108**.16, 17, 33
reasons for abusive behaviour **108**.2, 22
reporting to the police **108**.10, 36
types of abuse **108**.5–7, 24
domestic waste *see* household waste
domestic workers
children as **99**.1, 4, 7–10

doorstep recycling **111**.3, 29
doorstep selling and consumer rights **134**.20
dopamine **141**.9
doping *see* drugs in sport
dosage and drug effects **114**.2
Dove self-esteem fund **117**.13
Down's syndrome **60**.10
   and Alzheimer's disease **141**.7
   and learning disabilities **135**.33
DRC *see* Disability Rights Commission
Dreamers, The (film) **121**.24
drink-driving **119**.8–9; **143**.23–4
   alcohol limit **143**.3, 4
   and drugs **114**.23–4
Drinkaware Trust **143**.36
driver behaviour **119**.7–9
driving
   and alcohol *see* drink-driving
   and cannabis use **128**.14
   and disabled people **135**.4, 7
Drop the Debt protests **121**.14
droughts, and climate change **95**.5, 9, 11, 14, 15, 19,
     25, 26, 38
drug abuse **114**.1–30; **128**.11
   and HIV **96**.14, 26
   and homeless people **130**.11, 20
   parents' worries about **124**.17
   treatment **114**.10, 18–19
drug addiction **114**.17–19
drug development
   and animal experiments **103**.2–3, 9, 10, 11, 13
   use of stem cells **144**.18
drug overdoses **114**.5
   first aid **136**.23
   statistics **136**.26
drug testing **118**.25
   in schools **114**.26
   statistics **118**.33–4
   UK **118**.28, 30
   at work **128**.20
   World Anti-Doping Code **118**.31–2
Drug Treatment and Testing Orders **137**.12
drug treatments
   for depression **125**.7, 22, 32, 35
     manic depression **125**.19
     see also anti-depressants
   for gambling **129**.39
drugs
   and alcohol **143**.3, 10
   classification **114**.1, 31, 33
   definition **114**.1
   and dependency **141**.9
   depression caused by **125**.5–6, 10
   effects **114**.2, 29–30; **123**.8, 14
     crack **114**.10
     drug mixtures **114**.16–17
     ecstasy **114**.8, 29
     solvents **114**.27
   and families of drug users **114**.25
   getting help **123**.14
   market and prices **114**.6–7

and persistent offenders **137**.15
   risks **143**.21–2
   trade **114**.6–7, 11–12, 33–5
   and young people **114**.20–28; **123**.1–2, 8, 9, 14
drugs and the law **114**.31–9
   legalisation debate **114**.39
   classifications of drugs **114**.1, 31, 33
   prosecution and punishment **114**.32, 35, 36
   see also cannabis
drugs in sport **118**.23–39
   anabolic steroids **118**.35, 36
   androstenedione **118**.35
   athletes' responsibilities **118**.32–3
   beta-blockers **118**.37
   caffeine **118**.35
   cannabinoids **118**.38
   clenbuterol **118**.35
   consequences of abuse **118**.32, 24
   diuretics **118**.35, 37
   effects of drugs **118**.35–8
   ephedrine **118**.35
   erythropoetin **118**.35
   history of **118**.23–5
   hormones **118**.37
   medication and banned substances **118**.32–3
   nadrolone precursors **118**.35
   nalbuphine **118**.35
   narcotic analgesics **118**.38
   peptide hormones and analogues **118**.37
   pressure to take drugs **118**.28–9
   stimulants **118**.36–7
   see also drug testing
Dundee Paradise (cow) **144**.36–7
duty solicitors **137**.36

E

e-commerce, Europe **134**.15–16
e-learning **139**.28
e-mail
   bullying **122**.5, 19, 21
   personal emails in the workplace **104**.15
   phishing **104**.32–3; **134**.27–8, 28–9
   security measures **134**.28
   spam **82**.31–3, 36–7; **104**.30–1
   surveillance of
     and the Government **82**.1, 22, 23
     in the workplace **82**.25, 26, 27, 28, 30; **120**.32
E-number food additives and vegetarianism **140**.18
e-university **139**.28
early life crisis, men **112**.30
early medical abortion (EMA) 14, 33
earnings
   effect of education **139**.1
   graduates **139**.35, 36, 37
   minimum wage **107**.31
   teachers **139**.12
   see also incomes; salaries; wages
earnings gap **110**.16; **112**.16–17

ears, stem cell therapy **144**.22
eating disorders **117**.17–18; **123**.7, 33–4; **127**.1–31
    binge eating **117**.2, 15–16
    and body image **117**.27
    causes **117**.2–3, 6–7
    children **117**.3, 20–21
    and compulsive exercise **113**.38
    health risks **117**.4–5
    prevention programmes **117**.15, 18
    signs and symptoms **117**.2, 3, 17–19
        anorexia **117**.1, 2
        binge eating **117**.15, 16
        body dysmorphic disorder **117**.18–19
        bulimia **117**.1–2, 13, 14
    support for sufferers **117**.25–6, 28–30
    treatment **117**.28–9
        binge eating **117**.16
        bulimia **117**.14
        obesity **117**.34
    see also anorexia nervosa; bulimia nervosa; obesity
Eating Disorders Association (EDA) **117**.13, 22;
    127.21, 29
eating habits *see* diet; healthy eating
eco-systems
    degradation of freshwater **76**.35
    and water consumption **76**.2, 16–17, 19
eco-travel spending **134**.32
economic equality, Britain's ranking **112**.29
economic growth **98**.16
    Britain **134**.24
    and global warming **95**.9, 11, 16–17
    and poverty reduction **110**.29
economic hardship following divorce, effect on children
    124.34
economic inequality, and terrorism **92**.13, 21
economic migrants and homelessness **130**.19
economic wealth and cultural poverty **110**.23
economy
    and refugees **89**.21, 22, 30–1
    and tobacco **145**.22–3
ecotourism **109**.19–20, 38–9
ecstasy (MDMA) **114**.4–5, 8
    and depression **125**.10
    effects of **114**.8, 29
    mixed with other drugs **114**.16, 17
    possession of **114**.33
    prices **114**.6
    risks **143**.22
    users, influence of parenting style **114**.24
    young users **114**.22
ECT (electro-convulsive therapy) **125**.25–6, 34, 35
ectomorph body shape **127**.22
education **139**.1–39
    and alcohol **143**.20
    and behaviour problems in schools **120**.16
    body image improvement programmes **117**.15
    and black history **115**.16–17
    and black pupils **115**.19–21
    effects of cannabis use **128**.14
    and child labour **99**.3, 7, 15; **120**.18–19
    and child soldiers **99**.31

    and children's rights **120**.11
    costs **124**.3; **139**.1
    in developing countries **20**.20, 28
        costs **110**.38
    and disabled children **135**.24–5, **26**; 36–9
    and earnings **139**.1, 35, 36, 37
    and ethnicity **139**.8–9
    faith-based schools **94**.12–14, 28, 30–1
    and gender **112**.1–11; **139**.10–11
    global gender inequality **112**.39
    higher education **139**.29–39
    home learning **139**.27–8
    and homeless people
        level of education **130**.15
        needs **130**.34–5
    inequalities **110**.14
    and learning disabilities **135**.36–9
    in mental health **141**.37
    and minority ethnic pupils **115**.18
    in money matters **74**.1, 5–6, 12, 13
    and online learning **104**.9–10, 11
    and parents' mental health problems **141**.24
    PE **118**.3
    personal, social and health education **133**.16
    and racial integration **115**.29, 30, 37
    and racism **115**.19–20
    RE (religious education) **94**.9–10, 15, 31
    sex discrimination **112**.13–14
    about sexual abuse **132**.27
    about sexually transmitted infections **123**.25
    and smoking **145**.3
    and social mobility **139**.13
    special educational needs (SEN) **135**.36–9
    statistics **139**.1–2
    and teenage mothers **133**.24
    and war-affected children **99**.34
    and young people with HIV/AIDS **96**.26, 32, 33
    young people's attitudes to **123**.2
    and youth crime **137**.13
    see also educational achievement; schools; sex
        education; students; teachers; universities
Education Act and bullying **122**.11
educational achievement
    black pupils **115**.20
    and ethnicity **139**.8
    gender differences **112**.1, 8, 11
    and single-sex schooling **139**.11–12
    see also exam results
educational materials, gender equality **112**.9, 10
efficiency from reducing waste **111**.18
eggs
    consumer choices **140**.37–8
    free-range **140**.6, 29, 38–9
    from GM hens, and cancer treatment **138**.20–21
    and health **140**.30, 39
    production methods **140**.29, 38–9
    sales **140**.37–8
    and vegetarian diets **140**.6, 19, 26
elderly people
    and cancer **60**.3, 7, 14
    and dementia *see* dementia

and depression **125**.22–3
growth in numbers of **20**.9, 11
and homelessness **130**.17–18
and housing **85**.2, 10, 15
lesbian, gay and bisexual **101**.9–10
and mental health problems **141**.2
and poverty **110**.19–20
see also grandparents; older people
elections **131**.16–22
campaigns **131**.18
European **131**.15
General Elections **131**.18
terminology **131**.17
voter turnout **131**.19–21
electoral register **131**.16
electoral system **131**.15–26
electric hybrid vehicles **119**.22
electric vehicles **119**.21–2
electricity generation from waste **111**.39
electro-convulsive therapy (ECT) **125**.25–6, 34, 35
electronic equipment recycling **111**.31, 35
elephants
ivory trade **78**.20
killing of **78**.4, 6, 19
eliminating poverty **110**.23
Elliott, Michele **122**.6–7, 9–10
Ellis, Frank **121**.8, 9
ELVs, recycling **111**.35
embryo cloning *see* human reproductive cloning
embryo donors **144**.7
embryonic stem cell research **144**.2
ethical issues **144**.6
humanist view **144**.7–8
see also therapeutic cloning
embryos, hybrid **144**.9, 11, 14, 20
emergency contraception (EC) **126**.24
emergency treatment
for alcohol overdose **123**.16
self-harmers **136**.22–3
emissions, transport **119**.1, 15, 31
aircraft **119**.16
and climate change **119**.14, 24, 30
Emmaus Communities **130**.38–9
emotional abuse **108**.1, 6–7, 13, 19; **132**.1, 5–6
signs of **132**.4–5
emotional benefits of exercise **113**.22
emotional blackmail by parents **124**.15
emotional changes, and stress **100**.33
emotional damage caused by corporal punishment
132.10, 19
emotional disorders, young people **125**.9
emotional distress as cause of eating disorders **127**.2
emotional factors in obesity **113**.9
emotional health problems of consumerism **134**.5
emotional literacy classes **141**.37
emotional neglect in childhood, and low self-esteem
117.32
emotional problems, sharing **123**.10
emotional significance of food **113**.8
emotions
of animals **140**.27–8

and gender differences **112**.32–3
employees
gambling at work **129**.22–4
and Internet addiction **104**.37
and personal e-mail **104**.15
employers
and ageism in the workforce **105**.23–4, 26, 27
basic skills requirements **139**.17
equality policies **115**.13
liability for racism **115**.12
links with higher education **139**.38–9
and privacy rights in the workplace **82**.25–30
and sexual orientation monitoring **101**.24
and workplace stress **100**.17–18, 20
employment
and ageism **105**.4, 16–27
of disabled people **107**.12; **135**.3, 4, 14, 15
and gender **112**.12–27
graduates **139**.33
and homeless people **130**.15, 36–7
and lone parents **133**.28
and mental illness **141**.22
and obesity **113**.17
of parents as factor in child poverty **110**.12
and racism **115**.12, 13
students **74**.20, 29, 37; **139**.35
in urban areas in the developing world **20**.18, 19–20
working conditions **98**.4, 13, 14, 17, 25–6
see also hours of work part-time jobs;
unemployment; women in the workforce; work-
life balance; workplace
bullying; workplace stress
employment of refugees **89**.22–3, 24, 26–7, 32
illegal employment of refugees **89**.10–11, 30–1
employment rights and sex discrimination **112**.13
empty houses
and environmental decline **85**.14
numbers of **85**.25, 29
and the vacancy rate **85**.9, 25
ENCAMS (Environmental Campaigns) **111**.8
End Child Poverty coalition **110**.10
endangered species **78**.1–3
birds **78**.2, 8–9, 27, 29, 37
and climate change **95**.22
and the killing of wildlife **78**.2, 4–5, 5–6
mammals **78**.3, 27, 28, 32
plants **78**.2–3, 7, 17, 21, 36
and pollution **78**.6
trade in **78**.16–17, 19–22, 38–9
in the UK **78**.28–31
see also conservation; extinction; wildlife
endocrine disorders and depression **125**.5
endogenous (unipolar) depression **125**.4, 10
endomorph body shape **127**.22
energy
and the countryside **97**.24–5
and exercise **141**.39
and meat-eating **140**.21
and nutrition, teenagers **123**.6–7
output of the energy industry **97**.3
production and supply **97**.3–4

public attitudes to energy and environment 97.34–6
    saving through recycling 111.28, 30, 32
    from waste 111.2, 3, 39
energy consumption 97.6
energy efficiency 95.5, 28, 29–32; 97.27–33
    future of 95.28
    and global warming 97.29
    green electricity 95.32
    in the home 95.29, 30–1, 32; 97.2, 27–30, 31, 32–3
    in industry 95.34
    and renewable energy sources 97.11
    and shopping 97.31–2
    and sustainable housing 85.37
    and transport 95.5, 27, 28, 34; 97.24, 25, 31
    in the workplace 95.32
    see also renewable energy
Energywatch 134.21
engineering as career for women 112.27
England
    age of consent 133.1
    corporal punishment legislation 132.15
    flag 131.4
    Statutory Homeless households 130.13
    teenage abortion 133.2
    teenage pregnancy 133.2, 5
English people
    awareness of constitutional change 131.5
    British identity 131.6
Entertainment and Leisure Software Publishers Assoc.
    (ELSPA) 121.32–3
entrepreneurs 107.4
environment
    carbon dioxide emissions 98.14
    destruction, contributing to hunger 110.30–31
    and economic growth 98.16
    effects of genetic modification 138.12–14, 24
    and housing 85.14–15, 26
        see also sustainable housing
    information requests 142.19
    and meat production 140.13, 16–7
    and population growth 20.1, 4, 8, 22–4
        resource depletion 20.2, 3, 6
        water shortages 20.6, 9, 13–14, 22, 23, 24
    protection of 88.32, 34, 35
    public attitudes to 97.34
    use of resources to combat poverty 110.25–6
    and self-esteem 117.37, 38–9
    and tobacco 145.23
    and water bills 76.33, 34
    see also sustainable development; wildlife
environmental motoring, Ford 134.30
environmental tobacco smoke see passive smoking
Environmental Transport Association and congestion
    charging 119.34–5
environmentally cleaner vehicles 119.20–23
ephedrine 118.35
epidemiology (population studies) 103.17, 18, 19, 22
epilepsy and learning disabilities 135.34
equal opportunity in sport 118.12–13, 15–16, 18–19,
    22
equal pay 112.13, 20

gender pay gap 107.13, 25, 26; 112.16–17
Equal Pay Act 112.13
equality rights, disabled people 135.13
equity in sport 118.12
    gender equity 118.18–19
erythropoetin (EPO) 118.35, 37
escalation theory of drug use 114.39; 128.9–10, 11, 28
escharotics (cancer salves) 81.33
escort services for disabled people 135.9
estimates and consumer rights 134.18
ethical consumerism 134.30–38
ethical crime, Europe 137.6
ethical food 134.32, 34–7
ethical trade 98.3, 6; 134.36
    see also fair trade
ethical travel 134.30
ethics
    of genetic modification 138.23
    of human cloning 144.2–3, 5–6, 7–8
ethnic minorities
    British identity 115.38
    and community feelings 131.2
    and country of birth 131.8
    and education 115.18; 139.8–9
    and football 118.13–16
    and identity cards 82.2, 8
    interest in the news 142.32–3
    and mental illness 141.23
    mixed race population in the UK 115.24–5
    and national identity 131.1, 8
    and poverty 110.2
    and racial discrimination perception 131.2–3
    religious identity 94.3, 5
    and the UK census 115.3
    as victims of crime 115.10
    see also Asian people; black people; employment and
        racism; racism
ethnic origin
    and body image 117.29–30
    and child poverty 110.12
    and education 139.8–9
    as grounds for discrimination 115.7
    homeless people 130.10, 14
    young people and sex 123.19–20
ethnic stereotypes and reality TV shows 115.22
Europe
    alcohol trends 143.21, 31
    cannabis use 128.21–2
    online gambling 129.20
European Committee of Social Rights, and corporal
    punishment 132.17
European Convention on Human Rights and
    Biomedecine 144.11
European Union
    ban on advertising tobacco 145.7
    and biotechnology 138.28–9
    Charter of Fundamental Rights 120.27
    Charter of Fundamental Rights Related to
        Technological Innovation 142.1
    citizenship 131.38
    elections 131.15

GM ban, effect on developing countries **138**.29–30
GM Food and Feed Regulation **138**.11
and ID cards **131**.13
smoking **145**.21
students from EU countries **139**.30, 32
views of young people **131**.39
European Youth Parliament **131**.33
euthanasia
    active or direct **102**.1, 2
    and advance directives (living wills) **102**.18, 29, 32,
        33–9
    arguments against **102**.13–14, 28–9, 30–1
    arguments for **102**.12–13, 15
    and compassion **102**.12–13, 30
    defining **102**.1
    indirect **102**.1
    involuntary **102**.1
    law on **102**.5, 7, 8, 10, 15–16, 19
    and medical technology **102**.1, 3, 29, 30, 31
    non-religious perspective on **102**.1–2
    non-voluntary **102**.1
    and quality of life **102**.2, 29, 30
    religious views on **102**.2, 8–9, 12–14, 17, 18
    see also advance directives; assisted suicide; physician
        assisted suicide (PAS)
evidence obtained under torture **120**.39
evolution, and animals **78**.1
ex-prisoners, dangers of drug use **114**.14
exams **139**.4
    results
        A-levels **139**.18
        academies **139**.14, 15
        AS-levels **139**.18
        exceeding expectation **139**.22
        GCSEs **139**.2
        and single-sex schooling **139**.12
    standards **139**.19–20
    and stress **100**.3–7; **123**.29–30
        causes of **100**.5
        dealing with **100**.5, 6
        getting help and advice with **100**.3
    see also A-levels; AS-levels; GCSEs
Examzone website **139**.22
exclusion clauses and consumer rights **134**.19–20
exclusions from school
    black pupils **115**.19–20; **139**.9
    and ethnicity **139**.8, 9
exercise **88**.1, 2–3, 11, 12, 18; **113**.10, 21–30, 34–9
    aerobic exercise **113**.22
    barriers to **113**.25
    benefits of **113**.21, 22–3, 25, 30; **118**.3
        for women **118**.20
    children 113.1, 6, 8; **119**.31
    compulsive **113**.37–8
    and depression **113**.29–30; **125**.3, 20, 39
    and emotional health and wellbeing **113**.22
    and giving up smoking **145**.36
    and the heart **113**.34
    lack of *see* inactivity
    and life expectancy **105**.31
    and mental health **141**.34, 39

motivation for **113**.26, 35
recommended amounts **113**.22–3, 25–6, 27, 31, 37
    children **113**.1
and self-esteem **117**.37, 38
and stress
    benefits of **100**.19, 27, 30, 34, 36, 37
and weight reduction **113**.31
and young people **123**.2, 7
exercise referral **113**.30
exhaust gases *see* emissions, transport
exploitation of workers **120**.28–31
expression, freedom of *see* freedom of expression
extended warranties **134**.19
external costs of motoring **119**.14
extreme poverty **110**.21
    and Millennium Development Goals **110**.29
extremist parties **131**.23–4
    impact on democracy **131**.24
eyes
    stem cell therapy **144**.22
    test for Alzheimer's disease **141**.19

F

facial recognition technology **82**.3, 6, 17
    and identity cards **82**.9, 10
facial stem cell therapy **144**.21–2
factory farming and animal cloning **144**.35
fad diets **113**.33
FADS2 gene and ADHD **141**.19
fair trade **98**.3, 38; **109**.31; **110**.32–3; **134**.34–7
Fairtrade Foundation **134**.34–5, 36–7
Fairtrade mark **134**.35, 37
faith differences and relationships **115**.39
faith hate crime **115**.27
False Memory Syndrome **132**.34–5
families
    adjusting to a new family **124**.31
    and body image **117**.14
    and drinking behaviour of young people **143**.5, 17
    changing family patterns **106**.1–2; **124**.20–39
    and debt problems **74**.3, 5–6
    and disability **135**.4
    of drug users **114**.25
    family conflict and street homelessness **130**.10
    and football **141**.33
    holidays **110**.20
    of lesbians and gays
        coming out to **101**.2–3, 11, 12, 13
    and manic depressives **125**.20
    and obesity **113**.9
    pressure on athletes to take drugs **118**.29
    problems **124**.18
        young people's worries **123**.3
    reaction to mixed-faith relationships **115**.39
    and relationship support **106**.29–30
    size
        and child poverty **110**.13
        influenced by costs of raising children **124**.18

and working women **112**.20
and working parents **124**.1, 21
see also lone parents; parents; stepfamilies
family planning **20**.11, 25–40
    and the education of girls **20**.3, 9
    international conferences and programmes **20**.21,
        25–6, 28, 36–8, 39–40
    and maternal mortality **20**.25, 28, 29, 30
    and population growth **20**.3, 10
    and reproductive rights **20**.27–8, 35
    and sexual health **20**.27, 28, 33–5, 39–40
    and teenagers **133**.2
    US overseas aid restrictions **126**.19
    see also birth control; contraception
Farm Scale Evaluation (FSE) trials **138**.7, 13
farming *see* agriculture; organic farming
Fascism **92**.7
fashion, and the fur trade **103**.36–7
fast foods
    and litter **111**.12
fat intake **88**.2, 5, 7, 8
    in the diet **113**.14, 20
    and food labelling **88**.21–2, 22–3
    and red meat **140**.12
    teenagers **123**.7
fatalities *see* deaths
fathers
    and abortion **126**.13, 15–16
    and childcare **124**.7–11
    impact on children's achievement **124**.7
    employment patterns **107**.24–5
    full-time fathers **124**.9–10
    and household tasks **124**.11
    new fathers and depression **125**.14
    paternity leave **107**.25
    rights and responsibilities **133**.39
    teenage fathers **133**.25–7
    unmarried, and parental responsibility **124**.4
    working fathers **107**.24–25
fatty acids
    and ADHD (attention-deficit hyperactivity disorder)
        141.19
    in diet **141**.30
faulty goods, consumer rights **134**.17
favouritism by parents **124**.15
fear of crime **137**.5, 7
fear of terrorism **92**.3–5, 13
fear after traumatic bereavement **116**.11–12
fear of young people **137**.26–7
feelings
    of abuse victims **132**.22
    of animals **140**.27–8
    after bereavement **116**.1, 3–4, 5, 7–9, 10–11, 19,
        21–2, 30
    healthy self-esteem **117**.30
    low self-esteem **117**.5
fees, university **139**.34
female athlete triad **113**.23, 38
female condoms **123**.23
female health, Britain's ranking **112**.29
fertility

effect of abortion **126**.10
effect of smoking **145**.32
fertility genes, and homosexuality **101**.8
fetus
    abnormality and abortion **126**.9, 35
    development of **126**.26
    feeling pain **126**.22, 26
    rights **126**.21–2, 27
    viability **126**.27
fibre intake **88**.2, 5, 6, 23
file sharing **104**.39
films
    classification **121**.22, 23–5, 29–30
    cuts **121**.25
    and smoking **145**.8–10
    violence, and playground bullying **121**.28
final warnings, criminal offences **137**.12
financial abuse **108**.7, 15
    and older people **105**.13
financial benefits *see* state benefits
financial incentives for recycling **111**.34
financial pressure on athletes to use drugs 118.29
financial problems as cause of street homelessness
        130.11
financial products, expenditure on **134**.4
financial situations, women **112**.19
financial support to adult children
    by grandmothers **124**.38
    by parents **124**.3
financial worries and non-traditional families **124**.20
first aid **136**.22–3
    for drug emergencies **114**.30; **136**.23
first-time buyers, and house prices **85**.6, 7
fisheries, and climate change **95**.3, 7, 28
fishing **103**.30
    and globalisation **98**.14
    and the protection of the oceans **78**.14
fitness **113**.21, 24, 26, 27–8
    benefits of walking **113**.39
    and mental health **141**.34, 39
    motivation **113**.35
    young people **123**.2
    see also exercise
Fitness Industry Association (FIA) **113**.36
Five a Day campaign **123**.31
flags **131**.3–4
flashbacks
    drug use **114**.29–30
    about sexual abuse **132**.28
    after violent crime **137**.9
Fleet Street and newspaper publishing **142**.8–9
flexibility training **113**.23
flexible working **98**.17; **107**.2, 11–12, 14–19
    in an ageing society **105**.19–20, 27
    father-friendly employment **107**.25
    and gender equality **112**.20
    and lone parents **133**.38
    right to request **107**.17–18, 21–2
flooding
    and climate change **95**.1, 3, 5, 7, 9, 11, 12, 19, 38
    flash floods **95**.25, 38

impact of **95**.14, 25
    in the UK **95**.26
fly-tipping **111**.3, 9, 19, 20, 21
foetal alcohol spectrum disorder **143**.3, 33
foetal stem cells **144**.25
folate, increased in GM tomatoes **138**.14
food
    and alcohol **143**.7
    and animal cloning **144**.36–9
    and energy efficiency **97**.32, 33
    ethical **134**.34–7
    food value of alcohol **143**.2
    GM food *see* genetically modified (GM) crops
    hunger *see* hunger
    and mental health **141**.30–31, 34
    organic **134**.31
    and population growth **20**.2–3, 6, 8, 13, 24
    production and climate change **95**.1, 9, 11, 14, 15, 16
    production and global water supplies **76**.3, 4, 7, 18
    and religion **94**.10
    in schools, attitudes to **123**.32
    supplies in developing countries **20**.18, 24; **110**.30
    supplies and GM crops **138**.9, 10, 34–5
    and young people **123**.1
    see also diet; eating disorders; fast foods; fat intake;
        healthy eating; meat consumption; vegetarian food
food advertising and children **134**.10
food companies **98**.28–9, 30
food labelling **88**.9, 21–5
    GM food **138**.11, 39
food and nutrition **88**.1–39
    additives **88**.13–14, 34, 36, 38, 39
    advertising and promotion **88**.10, 11, 19, 20, 35, 37
    food poisoning **88**.14, 27–9
    food safety **88**.26, 32, 34
    healthy diet **88**.1–2, 5–7
    junk food **88**.9–11
    locally grown produce **88**.31, 33
    nutrition information panels **88**.21, 22–3
    teenagers **123**.6–7
    see also diet; healthy eating; nutrition; vegetarianism
food packaging **111**.11
food poisoning **88**.14, 27–9; **95**.28
food production
    and intensive farming **140**.36–7
    and meat consumption **140**.13, 16–17
    and mental health **141**.30
Food Standards Agency (FSA) and GM contaminated
        rice **138**.32
food weaknesses, Britain **113**.13–14
foot-and-mouth disease
    and the ban on hunting **103**.26
    and rural tourism in England **109**.25
football
    and disabled people **118**.22
    and homophobia **118**.17
    and mental health **141**.32–3
    racial equality **118**.13–16
    and violence **118**.7, 8
    wages **118**.11
Football Association (FA)

anti-homophobia campaign **118**.17
    and disabled supporters **118**.22
Football Foundation **118**.22
forced labour **120**.28–30
    children **120**.18–19
forced marriages **106**.15; **108**.24
Ford Motor Company, environmental concerns **134**.30
foreign investment **98**.17–18, 25
Foresight report **114**.14
forestry
    afforestation **95**.5
    and climate change **95**.2, 3, 4, 7, 15, 39
    forest fires **95**.4, 10
    regeneration of tropical rainforests **95**.2
    threatened species of animals in **78**.1, 2, 5
    see also deforestation
Formula 1 and tobacco advertising ban **145**.7
fossil fuels
    alternatives to reliance on **97**.2, 21
    as an energy source **97**.8, 21
    and biomass **97**.18
    burning **95**.2, 4, 6, 9, 10, 25, 38
    and energy efficiency **95**.20, 34
    see also oil
foster care, prohibition of corporal punishment **132**.15
fostering **133**.9
foundation schools **135**.36
foundation stage education, gender gap **112**.7
Fragile X syndrome **135**.33
France, online retail sales **134**.15
fraud
    and identity cards **82**.2, 7, 8, 11, 12
    phishing **134**.27
Freedom of Information Act **142**.18–20
    delays in meeting requests **142**.20
    and Doncaster Council **142**.21
    and regional newspapers **142**.17
Freedom Food mark **140**.29, 34
Freedom2Choose, challenge to smoking ban **145**.15
Freedom's Orphans: Raising Youth in a Changing World
        137.27
freight transport trends **119**.1
French Revolution, and terror **92**.1, 6–7, 10, 14
frequent offenders **137**.11, 15, 16
freshers' flu **123**.4
friends
    bullied, how to help **122**.13
    with eating disorders, how to help **127**.30
    as family **124**.19
    manic depressives, how to help **125**.20
    self–harmers, how to help **136**.16
friendship
    and football **141**.33
    and mental health **141**.28–9
    worries, young people **123**.3
fringe medicine *see* complementary medicine (CM)
fruit machines **129**.2
    and under 16s **129**.11
fruitarian diet **140**.2
FSA (Food Standards Agency) and GM contaminated
        rice **138**.32

fuel cell vehicles **119**.22–3
fuel efficient cars **119**.20–23
fuel taxes **119**.14, 24
    aircraft **119**.16
fuels, cleaner **119**.20–23
Fulham Football Club, and disabled supporters **118**.22
full-time fathers **124**.9–10
full-time mothers, working hours **124**.12
funding
    academies **139**.14
    BBC **142**.6
    students **139**.34–5
funerals **116**.3, 16, 20, 33–5
    alternative **116**.38–9
    arranging **116**.32
    children's questions about **116**.26
    environmental **134**.31
    and young people **116**.23
furnishings, spending on **134**.4
furniture recycling **111**.35–6
further education **139**.2

G

G8 protests **121**.14
GamAnon **129**.37
Gamblers Anonymous **129**.37
gambling **129**.1–39
    addiction *see* compulsive gambling
    addictiveness **129**.30
    benefits **129**.18
    controlled **129**.2, 28
    definition **129**.1, 28
    effects **129**.36
        physical **129**.29, 36
        psychological **129**.6, 29
        research **129**.16
    expenditure on **129**.4
        children **129**.32, 33
        mobile gambling **129**.26
        National Lottery **129**.9, 10
        online gambling **129**.17, 19
        Scotland **129**.32
        United States **129**.27
    forms of **129**.2
    Gambling Commission, The **129**.4–5
        licence conditions **129**.8, 23
    history of **129**.1
    and law
        Gambling Act **129**.5, 17, 23
        and gambling at work **129**.23
        online gambling **129**.17
    licensing **129**.5, 8, 23
    by mobiles **129**.18, 26
    and neurobiology **129**.6
    online gambling **129**.17–18, 19–25
    participation in **129**.4
        National Lottery **129**.9, 10
        online gambling **129**.19

young people **129**.11
problem gamblers *see* compulsive gambling
psychology of **129**.6, 29
signs of problems **129**.22–3, 24, 28, 29, 35–6, 38
social factors **129**.7, 29
statistics **129**.1–3, 4
underage **129**.1
    National Lottery **129**.11–13
    online gambling **129**.18, 25
    online poker **129**.25
    Scotland **129**.32–3
at work **129**.22–4
women **129**.21, 27, 34
young people **129**.1
    addiction **129**.25, 31, 32–3
    National Lottery **129**.11–13
    signs of gambling problems **129**.38
    views on gambling **129**.13
see also casinos; compulsive gambling; National
    Lottery
game as food source **140**.15
gammahydroxybutyrate *see* GHB
gangs and teenage safety **137**.20
gap years **107**.27
garden waste recycling **111**.16, 31, 33
gardens and water conservation **76**.1, 36, 37, 38
gateway effect, cannabis use **128**.9–10, 11, 28
gay men
    acceptance of **112**.38
    and anal sex **101**.3–4
    coming out **101**.11–13
    and depression **125**.15
    and the history of the LGBT community **101**.28–9
    and HIV **96**.17, 20, 23
    and the law **101**.5
        age of consent **101**.3, 9, 27
    and the media **142**.39
    and sexually transmitted infections (STIs) **96**.3, 4,
        10, 12
    see also homosexuality
GCSEs **139**.4
    academies **139**.14, 15
    and ethnicity **139**.8
    gender differences **112**.1, 8
    results **139**.2
GDP (Gross Domestic Product) **98**.14, 16
geep (sheep–goat chimera) 10
gender
    and ageism in employment **105**.22
    and alcohol consumption **143**.16, 31
    and alcohol effects **143**.7
    and alcohol limits **143**.27
    and bullying **122**.18
    and cannabis use **128**.22
    and car use **119**.29
    and child pedestrian accidents **119**.5
    of children and effects of divorce **124**.33
    and compulsive shopping **134**.14
    and depression **125**.2
    development **112**.28, 35
    and disability **135**.2

and education *see* gender and education
and employment **112**.12–27
homeless people **130**.10, 14
and life expectancy **105**.2, 9–10
and mental ill-health **141**.1
and online shopping **134**.16
and schizophrenia **141**.4
and self-harm **136**.7, 24, 26
and smoking **145**.1, 21, 22
children **145**.2, 5
and society **112**.28–39
and stress **100**.13, 19
and suicide risk **136**.33
victims of crime **137**.4, 7
young people in custody **137**.15
youth offenders **137**.14, 16
see also equal pay; men; women
gender-based violence **112**.39
see also domestic violence; rape
gender and education **112**.1–11; **139**.10–11
A-level performance **139**.18
and educational performance **112**.1, 8, 11; **139**.2
and examination results **112**.1, 8
higher education **112**.1, 8; **139**.32
subject choices **139**.11
vocational training **112**.1, 21–2
gender equality
and boys **112**.33–4
and careers options **112**.9, 20, 21–2, 23–7
in education **112**.9–11
and Oxfam programmes **112**.39
gender equity in sport **118**.18–19
gender gap
educational achievement **112**.1, 7, 8, 11
employment **112**.18, 20
international comparisons **112**.29
gender identity **101**.7
gender pay gap **112**.16–17
graduates **139**.36
gender stereotyping **108**.26; **112**.35
in education **112**.11
at work **112**.15
gender and work **112**.12–27
careers options **112**.9, 20, 21–2, 23–7
and equal pay **112**.13, 20
pay gap **112**.16–17
see also women in the workforce
general practitioners *see* GPs (general practitioners)
gene doping **118**.34
gene splicing *see* genetic modification
gene therapy **118**.39
General Elections **131**.18
genes **138**.4, 12
and addiction **141**.9
and attention-deficit hyperactivity disorder (ADHD) **141**.19
and depression **125**.2
and eating disorders **127**.6–7
fertility genes and homosexuality **101**.8
and obesity **113**.9; **127**.35
genetic barriers **144**.12

genetic engineering **144**.20
and the postponement of ageing **105**.31–3
genetic modification
definition **138**.1, 2, 4
and the environment **138**.12–14, 24
ethical issues **138**.23
limitations **138**.37–8
product labeling **138**.11, 25, 39
public attitudes to **138**.3, 15–16
technologies **138**.35
see also genetically modified crops; genetically modified organisms
Genetic Use Restriction Technologies (GURTs) **138**.18
genetically modified animals, experiments on **103**.1, 8, **144**.34
genetically modified (GM) crops **88**.14, 32, 33
and animal feed **138**.25
benefits of **138**.8–10
crop area **138**.2, 25, 29
cross-contamination **138**.6–7, 12–13
developing countries **138**.9, 10, 23, 29–30, 34–5
drug crops (pharming) **138**.4, 9–10, 20–22
and food production **140**.37
future for **138**.13
land register proposal **138**.36
non-food crops **138**.10, 14
potato research trials **138**.27, 28
rice **138**.20, 31–4
risks **138**.8–10, 24
safety **138**.6
tobacco plants **138**.21–2
UK **138**.2–3, 5, 39
genetically modified organisms (GMOs)
benefits **138**.12
concerns about **138**.12–13, 24
definition **138**.4, 12
hens **138**.20–21
see also genetically modified crops
genetics research **103**.11, 13
genital herpes **96**.3, 4
and HIV **96**.12
genital warts **96**.2–3, 4, 12–13
Genito-Urinary Medicine (GUM) clinics **96**.1, 10
health advisers and safer sex **96**.1, 10
and HIV testing **96**.16
pressure on services **96**.3, 4, 8–9, 11
and sexually transmitted infections **123**.25
tests and treatment offered at **96**.10
genomics **138**.2–3, 37–9
geospatial intelligence **120**.34
geothermal energy **97**.6–7, 9, 11–12
germ line therapy **144**.20
germ line transmission **144**.26
Germany
extremist parties **131**.23
migrant worker exploitation **120**.30–31
online retail sales **134**.15
germs **88**.27, 28–9
Getting it. Getting Right report **139**.9
GHB (gammahydroxybutyrate) **114**.31
and drug mixing **114**.17

ghettos **115**.28, 31
gifted and talented scheme, and black pupils **139**.9
girls' schools **112**.4–5
girls and young women
    academic achievement **112**.1, 8, 11
    and body image **117**.14–15, 19, 20–21, 22, 25
    and bullying **122**.10, 14, 15–16
    and child labour **99**.2, 3
    child soldiers **99**.29, 31, 36
    and cosmetic surgery **117**.26–8
    in developing countries **20**.25, 34
        education of **20**.3, 9; **110**.38
        and family planning **20**.29–30
    and dieting **117**.20–21
    and education
        examination results **112**.1, 8, 11
        foundation stage **112**.7
        single-sex teaching **112**.4–6
        vocational **112**.21–2
    and exercise
        overexercise **113**.23, 28
    and Internet access **104**.3
    and mental health problems **141**.1
    non-traditional career choices **112**
    and plastic surgery **117**.26–8
    and puberty **127**.22
    self-esteem programmes **117**.13, 15
    and self-harm **136**.7
    sexual behaviour **20**.26, 34
    sexual exploitation of **99**.16, 20, 21–2
    and smoking **145**.2, 5
    and sport **118**.20
    street children **99**.18–19
glaciers
    melting **95**.3, 7, 11, 14, 25, 26
glandular fever **123**.5
glass ceiling **107**.9; **112**.15–16, 20
glass cliff **107**.9; 112.20
glass recycling **111**.11, 23, 27, 28, 31, 36
global citizenship **131**.37
Global Gag Rule **126**.19
global gender inequality **112**.39
Global Initiative to End All Corporal Punishment of
    Children **132**.13
global nomads **109**.10
global positioning satellites and road charging **119**.36
global poverty **110**.21–39
    public opinions on **110**.34
global tourism
    and the air industry **109**.2
    destinations **109**.1
    growth of **109**.1–3, 7
    jobs created by **109**.1
global warming
    and air travel **109**.19
    causes of **95**.4, 9
    and changes in global climate zones **95**.14–15
    and consumer behaviour **134**.31
    effects of **95**.5, 6–7, 9, 11–15
    and energy efficiency **97**.29
    global temperatures **95**.5, 6, 7, 8, 9, 10, 11, 12, 35, 38

human influences on **95**.6, 25, 30, 33
    increase in **95**.2, 9, 10
    and population growth **20**.23, 24
    potential impact of **95**.2–3
    and renewable energy **97**.8
    see also climate change; energy efficiency;
        greenhouse gas emissions
globalization
    benefits **98**.1, 12
    and child labour **99**.14
    corporate globalisation **98**.25–7
    definition **98**.12
    effects of **98**.13–14
    and poverty **98**.1, 13, 35–6
    and the rich-poor gap **98**.33–4
    and unemployment **98**.19–20, 32, 37
'glorifying terrorism' offence **121**.9
glucose **88**.15
GM crops *see* genetically modified (GM) crops
GMOs *see* genetically modified organisms
GNVQs (General National Vocational Qualifications)
    139.4
gonorrhoea **96**.2, 3, 4, 8, 9, 10
    and HIV **96**.12
GoodBite (meat substitute) **140**.20
Google and Chinese censorship **121**.20–21
Government
    abortion time-limit review **126**.36–7
    control of the media **121**.1; **142**.2
    finance, and smoking **145**.1
    media censorship **121**.37
    media influence **142**.2
    Parliament **131**.15
    use of the media **121**.17–18
Government policies
    on age discrimination **105**.18, 20, 23–4, 26
    on child poverty **110**.2, 4, 6–7
    crime, public confidence in **137**.5
    on families
        children and divorce **106**.35–6
        and cohabitees **106**.7–8
        and marriage **106**.31
        and relationship support **106**.29–30
    on family holidays **110**.20
    on genetically modified crops **138**.5
    on homelessness **130**.16, 28, 33
    housing
        and the environment **85**.15
        in rural areas **85**.5, 27–8, 31
        social housing **130**.16, 33
    on ID cards **82**.7–12
    and the Internet
        child protection **104**.28–9
        closing the digital divide **104**.13
    on mental health in older people **105**.39
    sensible drinking guidelines *see* daily benchmarks on
        alcohol consumption
    on social exclusion **110**.8–9
    on surveillance **82**.1–3, 22, 23
    and women **110**.18
    on young people's health **123**.31

Government report on drugs trade **114**.11–12
Government targets
    child poverty **110**.2, 4, 6–7
    road safety **119**.4
GPs (general practitioners)
    and assisted suicide **102**.9, 15
    and bereavement support **116**.2
    and cancer **60**.31
        breast cancer **60**.22, 23
        childhood cancers **60**.10, 11
        diagnosis **60**.14
        in elderly people **60**.7
    and complementary medicine **81**.21, 29, 34
    and depression treatment for older people **105**.38
    and disability support **135**.4
    and eating disorders **127**.28
    reporting a death **116**.31
    seeking help for stress from **100**.2, 33, 34
    see also doctors
graduates **107**.14–15, 35–6
    basic skills concerns **139**.17
    construction industry **112**.25
    debt **139**.35
    earnings **139**.35, 36, 37
    employment **139**.33
    gender gap **112**.1, 8
    incentives for teacher training **139**.12
    starting salaries **74**.31; **139**.35, 36
grandparents
    and childcare **124**.1, 37–8
    opinions of parenting skills **124**.2
grants, student **139**.34
graves **116**.37
    visiting **116**.16
Greece, Ancient, sport and drugs **118**.23
Green Belt land **85**.28, 30, 31, 39
green burials **116**.39
green cars *see* fuel efficient cars
green exercise and mental well-being **117**.38
green space and mental health **141**.35
greenfield sites
    house-building on **85**.9, 25
    guidelines on **85**.28
    and housing density **85**.34
    and urban renewal **85**.35
greenhouse gas **111**.3
    see also carbon dioxide emissions
grief **116**.1–2, 3–5, 7–9
    counselling **116**.6
    importance of grieving **116**.3
    length of grieving process **116**.4–5
    public **116**.17–18
    and traumatic bereavement **116**.10–11
    and young people **116**.19–28
grooming, online **132**.33
Growing Schools initiative **123**.31
growth and nutrition, teenagers **123**.6–7
guarantees, consumer rights **134**.18–19
guilt, feelings after bereavement **116**.4, 11, 19
    children **116**.27
    and traumatic bereavement **116**.11

GURTs (Genetic Use Restriction Technologies) **138**.18
gym drugs **118**.35
gyms **113**.36
Gypsy/Roma children and education **115**.18

H

habitat loss
    and endangered wildlife in Britain **78**.30–1, 32
haematopoietic cell transplantation (HTD) **144**.21
hair, stem cell therapy **144**.22
hallucinogens **114**.2, 5, 29
happiness, increasing **117**.6
happy slapping **122**.5, 26
harassment **122**.30
    racial **115**.8
    sexual **112**.11
hard segregation **115**.28
hare coursing **103**.25, 26, 27
Hare Krishna (International Society for Krishna
    Consciousness) **94**.19
hashish (cannabis resins) **128**.1, 3, 6, 23
hazardous waste **111**.3
hazardous work
    and child labour **99**.1, 2, 3
    domestic labour **99**.7
headteachers, and homophobia **101**.38–9
health
    and alcohol **143**.4, 6, 7, 9–10, 27
    and cannabis **114**.37
        and the immune system **128**.19
        and lung cancer **128**.17, 19, 28
        respiratory effects **128**.18–19
        reclassification of **128**.30–32, 38
    and children's rights **120**.11
    and climate change **95**.1, 3, 7, 11, 15, 23, 27
    and cloning **144**.2, 6, 39
    and cycling **119**.39
    and eating disorders **127**.4–5
    and GM crops **138**.9–10
        see also pharming
    and homeless people **130**.20
        children **130**.23
        older people **130**.17
    male worries **112**.30
    and marriage **112**.38
    and meat consumption **140**.12, 13, 21
    and obesity **113**.5, 7, 10; **123**.31; **127**.32, 34
        in children **113**.7
    and older people **105**.3, 5, 28–39
    older people and health services **105**.6, 9
    and physical activity **113**.21, 22–3, 25, 29–30, 34;
        118.3, 20
    and poverty **110**.6, 35
    and self-esteem **117**.31, 33
    and smoking **145**.25–39
        benefits of giving up **145**.27, 35
        children **145**.2
        developing countries **145**.23

passive smoking **145**.2, 28–9
  and smoking ban **145**.12
students **123**.4–5
and traffic increase **119**.1
and traffic pollution **119**.13–14, 31
and underweight **113**.16
and vegetarian diets **140**.1, 2–3, 5, 11
and walking to school **113**.39; **119**.27, 31
worries, young people **123**.3
young carers **141**.24
see also mental health; mental illness
health care
  costs, obesity **127**.33–4, 37
  in developing countries **20**.18
  and disabled people **135**.4; 20
  information and the media **117**.18
  and masculinity **112**.37
  and refugees **89**.19–20
health cure scams **134**.27
health education on smoking **145**.3, 5
health warnings on alcohol **143**.30, 31, 32
healthy eating **88**.1–2, 5–7; **113**.8, 10, 32, 33; **127**.23
  children **113**.4, 5, 8
  as help for depression **125**.3, 39
  and meat consumption **140**.12, 14, 21
  and stress relief **100**.30, 31, 34, 35, 38–9
  and vegetarian diets **140**.1, 3–4, , 6, 7, 10, 11
  at work **113**.18
  young people **123**.1
  see also diet; food and nutrition
Healthy Schools Programme, National **123**.31
healthy weight maintenance *see* weight management
hearing, stem cell therapy **144**.22
heart attacks and cycling **119**.39
heart disease **113**.19–20
  and depression **125**.5
  and exercise **113**.34
  and eating disorders **127**.5
  and life expectancy **105**.2, 9, 10
  and medical research **103**.12, 18
  and obesity **113**.15
  and older people **105**.3
  protective effect of alcohol **143**.7, 27
  stem cell therapy **144**.22, 23, 28
  and stress **100**.19
heatwaves, and climate change **95**.25, 27, 28
Heavily Indebted Poor Countries (HIPC) initiative
  110.27
heavy drinking **143**.3, 8
  see also alcohol abuse
hemp **128**.6, 34
hens
  genetically modified **138**.20–21
  welfare **140**.38–9
  see also free-range eggs
hepatitis **103**.13
  and HIV **96**.10, 13
herbal cannabis (marijuana/grass) **114**.4; **128**.2, 3, 6, 23
  seizures of **128**.31
  see also sinsemilla; skunk
herbal medicine **81**.4, 11, 23, 36

banned herbs **81**.24
Chinese **81**.14–15
defining **81**.2, 11
effectiveness of **81**.24
expenditure on **81**.37
and multiple sclerosis **81**.30
and pharmaceutical drugs **81**.11
regulation of **81**.23
and scientists **81**.28, 29
herbicide tolerance **138**.4
heredity and mental illness **141**.24
heroin
  and cannabis use **128**.9–10
  mixed with other drugs **114**.16
  prices **114**.6–7
  smuggling **114**.34
herpes *see* genital herpes
hidden homelessness **130**.3, 13, 21–2
Hidden Lives report **135**.11
high blood pressure (hypertension) **88**.2, 9, 16
  benefit of exercise **113**.34
  and depression **125**.5
High Court **137**.36
higher education **139**.2, 29–39
  degree results **139**.33
  funding **139**.34
  statistics **139**.32
  see also further education; graduates; students;
  universities
Highers (exams) **139**.4
'highway code' for racial integration **115**.6
Hinduism **94**.6, 19, 21
  and abortion and contraception **126**.2–3
  beliefs **94**.2
  and the Census (2001) **94**.3, 5, 28
  festivals **94**.4
  food rules **94**.10
  funerals **116**.34
  and RE (religious education) **94**.9
Hippocratic Oath **102**.1, 14
hire purchase **134**.22
history, British, importance of teaching **131**.7
history of globalisation **98**.2
HIV (Human Immunodeficiency Virus) **96**.7, 14–39
  and babies **96**.31, 39
  and bacterial STIs **96**.12
  and child labour **99**.3
  and child soldiers **99**.31
  and children **96**.20, 39; **110**.37
  clinics **96**.10
  defining **96**.14
  in developing countries **20**.18, 20, 33
  drugs and recreational drugs **114**.16
  Government policies on **96**.16, 39
  and 'health tourism' **96**.21, 39
  and hepatitis **96**.10, 13
  increase in diagnoses **96**.8, 23, 39
  and parents of lesbians and gays **101**.17
  and population growth **20**.5
  prevention **96**.32–4

and condoms **96**.12, 14, 16, 24, 25, 29, 30, 32, 33, 34
    future of **96**.34
    and treatment **96**.32, 37, 38–9
prevention programmes **20**.25, 27, 28, 30, 37
and the sexual exploitation of children **99**.16, 24
signs and symptoms **96**.7
statistics **20**.36, 39
testing for **96**.1, 7, 8, 14, 16
transmission **96**.14, 18
treatments **96**.7, 14–15, 20–1
    antiretroviral therapy (ART) **96**.36, 37, 38, 39
    closing the treatment gap **96**.36–7
    combination therapy **96**.15
    costs of **96**.21
    drugs from GM (pharmed) crops **138**.21, 22
    and prevention **96**.32, 37, 38–9
    vaccines **96**.33–4
UK statistics **96**.20–2, 23
and unprotected sex **96**.12, 16, 28
and women **96**.17, 20, 24–5, 29, 30–1
    pregnant **96**.16, 22, 23, 31, 38
and young people **20**.34; **96**.17, 24–9, 38
    and alcohol and drug use **96**.26
    education **96**.26
    young women **96**.24–5, 27–8, 29
see also AIDS
Hodgkin's lymphoma **60**.4, 9, 10
holidays
    and bullying **122**.12
    ethical **134**.30
    expenditure on **134**.3
    low income families **110**.5, 20
    see also responsible tourism
holism **81**.2
Holocaust denial **121**.8, 12–13
home abortions **126**.32–4
home expenditure, ethical **134**.32
home furnishings, spending on **134**.4
home learning **139**.27–8
home schooling **139**.27
home and sex education **133**.15
Home-Start volunteers **124**.6
homeless households **85**.11; **130**.1
homeless young people **130**.14–15, 21–7
    and debt **130**.24–6
    hidden homelessness **130**.21–2
    homelessness causes **130**.21
    mental health **130**.27
homelessness
    and affordable housing **130**.8, 16, 23, 33
    and beggars **130**.12
    causes **130**.3, 6, 10–11
        young people **130**.21
    and children **130**.23
    defining **130**.1–3
    and drug use **130**.11, 20
    and employment **130**.15, 36–7
    and health **130**.20
        children **130**.23
        older people **130**.17

government strategies **130**.16, 28, 33
help for homeless people **130**.21–2, 28–39
hidden homeless **130**.3, 13, 21–2
history of **130**.4
intentionally homeless **130**.
legislation
    England and Wales **130**.28
    Scotland **130**.5
and local authorities **130**.2–3, 28, 29–30
and mental health problems **130**.20
    street homeless **130**.11
    young people **130**.27
myths and facts **130**.7
and older people **130**.17–18
preventing **130**.28–30
priority needs homeless **130**.2
reduction in **130**.16
repeat homelessness **130**.34
risk factors **130**.3
rough sleeping **130**.6, 9–12
Scotland **130**.5–6
statistics **130**.13–15, 22
see also homeless young people; street homelessness; temporary accommodation
homeopathy **81**.12–13, 23, 36
    and cancer **81**.32
    defining **81**.2, 12
    effectiveness of **81**.22, 24, 28
    expenditure on **81**.37
    and the placebo effect **81**.26
    and scientists **81**.28–9
    treatments **81**.12–13
homework **139**.27, 28
homeworking **107**.12, 14–15, 19–20, 22
    scams **134**.27
homicide **137**.7
    and domestic violence **108**.7
    see also murder
homophobia
    in football **118**.17
    hate crime **101**.29, 36–7
    homophobic bullying **101**.3, 13, 18, 19, 20, 21–2, 38–9; **122**.3
    and male friendships **112**.34
    and mental health problems **101**.20
    and violence **137**.8
homosexuality
    acceptability of **112**.38
    and ageing **101**.9
    awareness of **101**.14–15
    and Christianity **101**.5–7, 15, 18, 29
    coming out **101**.11–13
        in the workplace **101**.23–4
    'correction' of **101**.5–6, 10
    equality struggles **101**.9
    and genes **101**.8, 14
    history of the LGBT community **101**.28–9
    and the law **101**.3, 10
    and the media **142**.39
    same-sex partnerships and the law **101**.30–2

and section 28 of the Local Government Bill **101**.28–9
    repeal of **101**.18, 21, 22, 29, 39
  and young people **123**.21; **133**.2
hooliganism, football **118**.7, 8
Honeyford, Ray **115**.33
honour crimes **108**.24
hormonal methods of contraception **123**.23
  see also pill, contraceptive
hormones
  and appetite regulation **127**.38–9
  use in sport **118**.37
horse meat as food **140**.18
hospice care **60**.8, 13; **102**.3–4, 13, 28, 31
hospitals
  admission for manic depression **125**.19–20
  admission for self-harm **136**.4, 10
  death, formal procedures **116**.31
  female consultants **112**.26
hostels **130**.31
hours of work **107**.2, 3, 6, 14, 24
  fathers **124**.11
  full-time mothers **124**.12
  inequality **110**.14
  see also employment
House of Commons **131**.15
House of Lords **131**.15
house prices **85**.1, 3–4; **134**.25
  and first-time buyers **85**.6, 7
  and homelessness **130**.8
  regional differences in **85**.3–4, 6, 8
  and single people **85**.7
household crime **137**.4
  racial identity of victims **115**.10
household tasks and working parents **124**.11
household waste **111**.3
  composition of **111**.22
  food packaging **111**.11
  kerbside collections of **111**.3, 29
  microchip analysis **111**.38
  prevention **111**.16
  recycling **111**.6
  see also composting waste; waste management
households
  and energy efficiency **95**.29, 30–1; **97**.2, 27–30, 31,
    32–3
  expenditure patterns
    and older people **105**.5
  growth in numbers of **85**.1–2, 3, 29
    and the need for new homes **85**.8–9, 20
  income gap **110**.16
  low income **110**.12–13
  size of **106**.2, 3
  structure and child poverty **110**.12–13
  see also families; homeless households
housework
  and men **112**.30
  parents, time spent on **124**.11
housing
  advice centres **130**.29
  age of houses in the UK **85**.30

and child poverty **110**.12
debt **134**.23
and the environment **85**.14–15, 26
expenditure **134**.4
home ownership in the UK **85**.30
housing crisis 'backlog' **85**.2
investment in as a share of gross domestic product
  85.3
in London **85**.10–13, 16–17
and lone parents **133**.37
need for new homes **85**.1–3, 8–9
  numbers required **85**.9, 20
  and planning laws **85**.20
  targets **85**.1
and 'neighbourhood collapse' **85**.38
new house-building
  in cities **85**.25
  and housing density **85**.25, 34
  in the M11 region **85**.18, 22, 26, 27, 33
  numbers being built **85**.3
  and planning permission **85**.35
  in the Thames Gateway **85**.21–4, 26, 33
and older people **105**.6
rented accommodation shortage **130**.8
and same-sex partnerships **101**.31
and sex discrimination **112**.14
shortage **130**.8, 16, 30
size of houses in the UK **85**.30
social housing
  shortage **130**.8, 23
  Government strategy **130**.16, 33
and urban growth in developing countries **20**.17–18
see also affordable housing; homelessness; rural
  housing; temporary accommodation
housing associations
  and house–building **85**.24
  in London
    and shared ownership houses **85**.11
    and unfit dwellings **85**.12
  and private developers **85**.19
Housing Benefit **133**.34–5; **135**.5
  problems, and homelessness **130**.9
HTML (Hypertext Markup Language) **104**.2
human-animal embryos **144**.9, 11, 13, 14, 20
human-ape hybrids **144**.11
human cloning **144**.1–14
  ethical issues **144**.2–3, 5–6, 7–8
  public attitudes **144**.35
human dignity
  and cloning **144**.3
  and inter-species mixing **144**.12
human embryos
  stem cells *see* embryonic stem cells
  hybrid embryos **144**.9, 11, 13, 14, 20
Human Fertilisation and Embryology Act **126**.8;
  144.15, 27
Human Fertilisation and Embryology Authority
  (HFEA) **144**.14, 17
human genes
  in bacteria **144**.11
  in mice **144**.11

see also hybrid embryos
human growth hormones (HGHs) and sport **118**.37
human reproductive cloning
    autonomy issues **144**.3
    benefits **144**.2
    and dignity **144**.3
    ethical concerns **144**.2–3, 8
human rights **98**.29, 38; **120**.23–7
    and animal rights **103**.33
    and cartoons of Mohammed **121**.11–12
    and CCTV **82**.24
    and child labour **99**.4, 6
        domestic work **99**.8
    and child soldiers **99**.30, 31–2
    and children's rights **120**.1–22
    and corporal punishment **132**.9, 12–13, 16–17
    and euthanasia **102**.13
    and identity cards **120**.37
    and privacy **82**.4–5, 18
    and refugees **120**.31
    smoking ban challenge **145**.15
    and surveillance **120**.33
    and terrorism **92**.25
    water as a human right **76**.24–5, 32
    and workers **120**.28–31
Human Rights, Universal Declaration of **120**.23–5
Human Rights Act **82**.18, 24, 39; **94**.29; **108**.38–9;
    120.25–7
    and workplace monitoring **82**.29; **120**.33
Human Rights Committee, and corporal punishment
    132.17
humanism
    and abortion **126**.4–5
    and animal welfare **140**.31–3
    and embryo research **144**.7–8
    and euthanasia **102**.1–2
    and faith-based projects **94**.16
    and faith-based schools **94**.31
    funerals **116**.35
    and the Golden Rule **94**.11
    and 'incitement to religious hatred' **94**.32
    and the law on freedom of religion or belief **94**.29
    and RE (religious education) **94**.9, 15
    and religious diversity **94**.38–9
hunger
    developing world **110**.31–2
    Millennium Development Goals **110**.30–31
hunting **103**.24–31
    arguments against **103**.26
    arguments for **103**.24–5
    badger digging **103**.28
    before the ban **103**.26
    for bushmeat **78**.18
    clothes worn **103**.25
    and the control of wild animals **103**.25
    and cruelty **103**.25, 26
    deer hunting **103**.24, 28
        with helicopters **103**.29
    draghunting **103**.24–5, 26
    as food source **140**.17
    fox numbers and the ban on **103**.26

and Globally Threatened Birds **78**.8
hare coursing **103**.25, 26, 27
history of the abolition of **103**.27–8
and hounds **103**.24
hunt saboteurs **103**.28, 30
killing the fox **103**.24
law on (Hunting Act 2004) **103**.26, 27
    testing enforcement of **103**.31
and mammals in the UK **78**.32
otter hunting **103**.28
public attitudes to **103**.24, 25
questions and answers on **103**.24–5
whales **78**.6, 13, 14
of wildlife **78**.2, 4–5, 5–6
Huntingdon's disease **141**.6–7
hybrid animals **144**.10–12
hybrid embryos **144**.9, 11, 13, 14, 20
hybrid vehicles **119**.22
hybridisation **138**.12–13
    see also cross-contamination; cross-pollination
hydrocarbon (HC) emissions **119**.15
hypertension *see* high blood pressure

I

ice sheets
    melting **95**.3, 5, 8, 12–15, 24, 33, 39
ICT (Information and Communication Technologies)
    and online learning **104**.9–10, 11
identity
    British identity of non-white ethnic groups **115**.38
    protection in interviews **142**.12
    racial, victims of crime **115**.10
    religious **115**.5, 26
    social identity and football supporters **141**.32–3
identity (ID) cards **82**.1, 2, 7–12; **120**.34, 35–6;
    131.13–14
    and biometric data **82**.9, 10, 12
    and bogus asylum seekers **82**.7, 8
    and civil liberties **82**.11–12
    and electronic fraud **82**.11
    fee to be charged for **82**.7, 8, 10
    fraud **82**.7, 8
    and health and welfare benefit abuse **82**.7, 8, 9
    and human rights **120**.37
    and identity fraud **82**.11, 12
    opposition to **82**.7, 8
    and personal freedom **82**.8
    public attitudes to **82**.7–8
identity disorders **141**.11
identity theft **134**.27–8, 28–9
illegal broadcasting **142**.7
illegal drugs trade **114**.33–5
illegal dumping *see* fly-tipping
illegal employment **89**.10–11, 30–1
illegal immigrants **89**.11, 30–1
illegal parking **119**.9
illegal planting of GM crops **138**.19
illness and depression **125**.2, 5–6

images, effects on young people's behaviour **145**.6

IMF (International Monetary Fund) and world debt **110**.27

immigration

illegal immigrants **89**.11, 30–1

and population growth **20**.4–5, 11, 15–16, 32

quota system proposal **131**.10

see also asylum seekers; ethnic minorities

immune system, effect of cannabis **128**.19

immunisation

and animal diseases **103**.12

and life expectancy **105**.2

imports **98**.1, 9

imprisonment *see* prison

Improving the Life Chances of Disabled People **135**.23–4

in vitro (in glass) research **103**.14, 18, 19

inactivity

children **113**.7, 8

and coronary heart disease **113**.20

Incapacity Benefit **135**.5

incentives for recycling **111**.34, 37

incest **132**.26

incineration **111**.3, 6, 22

disadvantages **111**.7, 15, 22

inclusion

and sport **118**.12

disabled people **118**.22

ethnic minorities **118**.13–16

women **118**.18–22

inclusive education **135**.37–9

and behavioural problems **120**.16

Income Support **133**.33; **135**.5

incomes **98**.5, 13, 18, 32, 33; **107**.2, 13

inequality of

global **110**.35

UK **110**.13, 14, 16

minimum wage **107**.31

lone-parent families **124**.35; **133**.28, 30

older people **105**.4–5

and older women **105**.21

and part-time working **107**.17

stress and income levels **100**.13

and voter turnout **131**.19

women **110**.17–18

young people **110**.10

see also earnings; equal pay; salaries; wages

incontinence and stem cell therapy **144**.21

independence, encouraging children's **124**.13–14

Independence Day report **135**.20

independent holidays **109**.8–9

independent living and learning disabilities **135**.34–5

independent schools and SEN provision **135**.36

Independent Television Commission (ITC) **121**.36

index of isolation **115**.32

index of segregation **115**.31–2

indirect euthanasia **102**.1

indirect racial discrimination **115**.7, 11

indirect sex discrimination **112**.13

indoor (contained) GMOs **138**.12

Industrial Injuries Disablement Benefit **135**.5

Industrial Revolution and sport **118**.24

industrial waste disposal **111**.24

industrialisation

and climate change **95**.3, 9

and population growth **20**.2

industry

and child labour **99**.1, 2

and energy efficiency **95**.34

motivations for GM development **138**.8

water consumption **76**.2, 8, 36

water pollution **76**.11

inequality

gender *see* gender gap

and globalisation **98**.5, 13, 33–4

of incomes **110**.13, 14, 16, 35

and segregation **115**.30, 31, 32

social **110**.14

and terrorism **92**.13, 21

see also child poverty; poverty

Infant Life Preservation Act **126**.7

infant mortality **20**.28, 29, 30, 31

infection risk of abortion **126**.14

infections

as cause of anorexia **127**.12

as cause of depression **125**.5

infertility

and anti-abortion movement **126**.25

information

children's rights to **120**.10

as consumer right **134**.1–2

for disabled children **135**.21

and ethical consumerism **134**.33–4

see also Freedom of Information Act

information technology (IT)

educational projects **82**.28

and globalisation **98**.4

see also computers

Information Tribunal **142**.19

inherited learning disability **135**.33

injectable hormonal contraceptive **123**.23

injury prevention and exercise **113**.28

inner city areas, voter turnout **131**.19

inquests **116**.32

insects, GM viral infections **138**.13–14

insecurity

and bullying **122**.8

feelings after bereavement **116**.4

Inside-Out Trust **137**.2

insomnia

and stress **100**.19, 29

instant justice by police, proposal **137**.34

instant messaging (IM) and bullying **122**.20, 21

institutional disablism **135**.28

institutional prejudice in childhood, and low self-esteem **117**.32

institutions, leaving, as cause of homelessness **130**. 11

instructions to discriminate **115**.12

insulin, effect of nicotine **145**.26

insurance

car insurance offences **119**.9

and homeworking **107**.20

life insurance **106**.14
  and money management **106**.14
  and privacy rights **82**.25–6
  and sustainable tourism **109**.28
  and young people **74**.2, 15
  and young travellers **109**.11, 12, 13, 14–15
integrated medicine/healthcare **81**.36–8
integration, racial *see* racial integration
intellectual property rights **98**.21, 22
  see also patents
intelligent speed adaptation technology **119**.18
intelligent transport systems **119**.38
Intensive Supervision and Surveillance Programmes
  (ISSP) **137**.12
intentionally homeless people **130**. 2
inter-ethnic marriages **115**.25
  see also mixed-race relationships
inter-species mixing **144**.10–12
interactive gambling **129**.17–26
interest free credit **134**.22
interest rates
  credit cards **74**.26, 27
  and mortgage repayments **85**.6
  and savings **74**.24
interests, and improving self-esteem **117**.6, 8, 33
Intermix, website for mixed-race families **124**.36–7
internally displaced persons **89**.1, 6, 8–9
international anti-doping policy **118**.27–8, 31–2
International Labour Organisation and child labour
  120.20
international law and child labour **120**.20
International Monetary Fund (IMF) and world debt
  110.27
International Obesity Taskforce **113**.12
International Olympic Committee (IOC), anti-doping
  initiatives **118**.25
international students **139**.30, 31, 32
international trade **98**.4, 21–3
  and genetic modification **138**.27
  and poverty **110**.22, 30
  see also globalisation
Internet
  addiction **104**.36–7; **142**.37
  banking **74**.2; **104**.12
  broadband access **104**.3, 12
  bullying by e-mail **122**.5, 19, 21
  cafés **104**.14
  and censorship **121**.18–21
    China **121**.2, 19–20
  and child sex abuse **132**.30, 31–2, 33
  and children and young people **104**.3–5, 9–11
    access **104**.3, 13
    and chat rooms **104**.5, 20–1
    nature of use **104**.3–4
    online communication **104**.4–5
    online learning **104**.9–10, 11
    and parents **104**.4, 9–10
    and safety **104**.17–29; **132**.33
    statistics **104**.3–5
  and divorce rates **106**.31
  etiquette **104**.1, 35

file sharing **104**.39
fraud **134**.26–9
gambling *see* online gambling
instant messaging **104**.35
journalism register **142**.16
and media regulation **142**.2
movie-swapping **104**.38–9
National Lottery games, and under 16s **129**.12–13
as news source **142**.33
and newspapers **142**.9
non-users **104**.15
and older people **105**.8, 11
online bullying **122**.19–26
phishing **104**.32–3; **134**.27–8, 28–9
public attitudes to Internet use **104**.15
regulation **142**.2
sex offenders, helpline for **132**.36
and the sexual exploitation of children **99**.16, 21, 24
shopping **104**.5–8
  Europe **134**.15–16
  and gender **134**.16
social networking sites **142**.35, 36, 38
suicide websites **136**.37, 38, 39
surveillance
  and the Government **82**.1, 22, 23
  in the workplace **82**.25, 26, 27, 28; **120**.32
travel industry **109**.6
what it is **104**.1
see also child pornography; e-mail; safety and the
  Internet; websites
Internet Protocol (TCP/IP) **104**.2
Internet Service Providers (ISPs) **104**.1
  and child pornography websites **104**.29
  and spam **104**.30, 31
Internet Watch Foundation (IWF) **132**.31–2
intersexuality **101**.7
intestinal problems and eating disorders **127**.5
Invalid Care Allowance **135**.5–6
investment scams **134**.27
involuntary euthanasia **102**.1
involuntary smoking *see* passive smoking
iodine and vegetarian diet **140**.3
IQ
  gender differences **112**.31
  and post traumatic stress disorder **141**.3
  and vegetarian diet **140**.10
IRA (Irish Republican Army) **92**.2, 11, 23; **94**.10
Ireland, Northern
  age of consent **133**.1
  and corporal punishment **132**.15, 16
  self-harm statistics **136**.26
  teenage pregnancy **133**.2, 5–6
  teenage sexual behaviour **133**.1–2
iridology **81**.17–18
iris recognition, and identity cards **82**.9, 10, 11, 12
iron in the diet **88**.6, 15
  red meat **140**.12
  sources **140**.4, 7
  teenagers' needs **123**.6
  and vegetarian diet **140**.1, 3, 7
irrigation

and global water supplies **76**.3, 4, 5, 19
and water shortages **76**.21
Irving, David **121**.8
Islam
and abortion and contraception **126**.2
and the Census (2001) **94**.3, 5, 28
festivals **94**.4, 35, 36
five pillars of **94**.3–4
food rules **94**.10
funerals **116**.34–5
Golden Rule **94**.8, 11
and 'honour killings' **94**.30
media treatment of **94**.33
Muslim schools **94**.12, 13, 14
new religious movements/cults **94**.19, 21, 25
and RE (religious education) **94**.9, 31
and terrorism **92**.13
condemnation of **92**.26, 28–9, 37–8
convictions of Muslims in the UK **92**.27
tradition and beliefs **94**.2
Islamophobia **115**.36
and national identity **131**.11

Jainism **94**.2
Jamaica, ideal female body shape **117**.30
Japan, suicides **136**.39
Jehovah's Witnesses **94**.1, 19
Jews
and abortion and contraception **126**.3
beliefs **94**.2, 4
and the Census (2001) **94**.3, 5, 28
festivals **94**.4
food rules **94**.10
funerals **116**.33–4
Jewish schools **94**.30
and racism laws **115**.26
and RE (religious education) **94**.9
terrorist groups **92**.2–3
in first-century Palestine **92**.1, 6
job hunting **107**.31–2
job prospects and obesity **113**.17
job satisfaction **107**.1–2, 13
women **112**.22–3
job security **98**.5; **107**.1, 2
Jobseekers Allowance **133**.33–4
journal keeping as way of remembrance **116**.16
journalists
and libel law **142**.27
protection of sources **142**.22
regulation **142**.16
talking to **142**.11–14
journey length trends **119**.29
travelling to school **119**.30
Jubilee Debt Campaign **110**.27
judiciary, women in **112**.18
junk food advertising, effect on childhood obesity **113**.2
junk mail **111**.5; **134**.26, 28

justice system and children **120**.12
Jyllands-Posten newspaper **121**.10, 11, 15

Keep Britain Tidy campaign **111**.8, 12
keeping fit *see* fitness
Kenya and the Global Gag Rule **126**.19
ketamine **114**.3, 31
and drug mixing **114**.17
and drugs market **114**.6
kerbside recycling **111**.3, 29
Key Stages (schools) **139**.1–2, 5
key workers
affordable housing for **85**.1, 3, 20
in the Thames Gateway **85**.21, 22, 23
see also public sector workers
khat and the law **114**.31–2
Kick it Out, anti-racism campaign **118**.14
kidnapping, by terrorists **92**.9
kidney cancer **60**.5, 16, 17
in childhood **60**.9, 11
kidney damage and eating disorders **127**.5
Killing with Kindness campaign **130**.32
killings *see* homicide; murder
kinesiology **81**.2
kitchen waste **111**.31, 33
knee repair, stem cell therapy **144**.21
knife carrying by young people **137**.16

labelling
alcohol **143**.30, 31, 32
ethical products **134**.34
GM animal feed **138**.25
GM food **138**.11, 39
and low self-esteem **117**.6
products **134**.1–2
labour costs **98**.13
labour market
and tourism **109**.32
and women **112**.12
working conditions in the tourist industry **109**.30, 31, 32
Labour Party, policies on crime **137**.2
lacto-ovo-vegetarians **140**.2
lacto-vegetarians **140**.2
lactose, and vegetarians **140**.19
lads' magazines **142**.29
lager, strength of **143**.1
landfill **111**.3, 5, 6, 22
problems **111**.7, 15, 22
tax **111**.3, 7
landlord support services **130**.29
language
in advertising **134**.9
barriers to employment **89**.27, 35, 37

in schools and gender equality **112**.10
    strong language on television **121**.38–9
lanolin, and vegetarians **140**.19
laughter as help in grieving **116**.13
law *see* legislation
law-making process **131**.24
    citizen involvement **131**.25
Lawrence Report (Macpherson Inquiry) **115**.8
laxatives, effects **127**.2
leachate **111**.3, 15
leadership in sport
    ethnic minorities **118**.13
    women **118**.20
leadership skills development, women **112**.15–16
leakage, and the tourist industry **109**.32–3
Learndirect **139**.28
learning
    effects of cannabis **128**.14
    impact on homelessness **130**.34–5
    and older people **105**.5
    online **104**.9–10
learning disabilities **135**.33–9
    causes **135**.33
    definition **135**.33
    management of **135**.34–5
    and the media **135**.35
    and education **135**.36–9
    see also disabled people
Learning and Skills Council **139**.4
leaving home *see* domestic violence, leaving home
legal advice and court hearings **137**.26
legal rights, young people **120**.7–8
legal status of drugs **114**.1
legislation
    and abortion **126**.5, 6, 7–8, 12
    and alcohol **123**.16; 2–3
        drink-driving **143**.24
        young people **143**.2, 17
    on asylum **89**.3–4, 11, 12, 33, 39
    blasphemy **121**.16
    and bullying **122**.11
        racist bullying **122**.4
    and cannabis **128**.2, 7, 9, 26–38
    Communications Act and media mergers **142**.4
    and corporal punishment **132**.8, 15–17
    on crime **137**.21, 29–30
    and drugs *see* drugs and the law
    on embryo research **144**.15, 17, 27–8
    and film classification **121**.23–5
    on food additives **88**.39
    on food labelling **88**.23, 24, 25
    Freedom of Information Act **142**.17–21
    on gambling
        Gambling Act **129**.5, 17, 23
        and gambling at work **129**.23
        online gambling **129**.17
    on homelessness
        England and Wales **130**.28
        Scotland **130**.5
    law-making process **131**.24
        citizen involvement **131**.25

libel and journalistic freedom **142**.27
libel and slander **142**.26
on littering **111**.9, 19
protection from domestic violence **108**.38–9
Racial and Religious Hatred Bill **121**.7, 15
and racism **115**.2, 7–8, 26
    at work **115**.11–12
on religious hatred **115**.26; **121**.7, 15
and smacking **132**.8
and smoking
    ban on smoking in public places **145**.11–17
    children **145**.3
    young people **123**.12
and video **121**.31
video games classification **121**.32
on waste treatment **111**.2
leisure
and older people **105**.5, 28
Leonard Cheshire Disabled People's Forum **135**.15
leptin (appetite-suppressing hormone) **127**.39
lesbians
and bullying in schools **101**.19
and the history of the LGBT community **101**.28–9
and homophobic bullying **101**.3
issues facing young women **101**.19–20
and the law **101**.3, 10, 27, 28
 and the media **142**.39
and sexually transmitted infections **101**.4
and workplace discrimination **101**.23, 24
see also homosexuality
leukaemia **60**.5, 9, 16, 17, 33
bone marrow transplants for **60**.35
childhood **60**.9, 10, 12
and medical research **103**.12
stem cell therapy **144**.21
Level Playing Field campaign **118**.22
liability for racism at work **115**.12
Lewy bodies (dementia) **141**.7
libel **142**.26
and journalism **142**.27
Liberal Democrat Party, policies on crime **137**.2
liberalisation **98**.2–3, 9, 23
licence fee, BBC **142**.6
licensing
alcohol sales **143**.2
gambling **129**.5, 8, 23
hybrid embryo research **144**.14
stem cell research **144**.17, 27–8
licensing hours and crime **143**.23
Life (Save the Unborn Child) **126**.7, 38
life chances
effect of child poverty **110**.7
and teenage parenthood **133**.10
life expectancy **98**.12
and AIDS **20**.3, 5, 11
and alcohol consumption **143**.13
in developed regions **20**.5
and gender **105**.2, 9–10
increase in **105**.35
    reasons for **105**.1–2
in less developed regions **20**.5, 18

and smoking **145**.21
ways of increasing **105**.29–31
lifestyle
and life expectancy **105**.2, 9–10, 36
and obesity **113**.6, 7, 9
in children **113**.1, 2
and older people **105**.34
sedentary lifestyles, children **113**.1, 7, 8
sports **118**.1
stress and changes in **100**.19
light therapy for Seasonal Affective Disorder **125**.18,
37; **141**.35
lip cancer **60**.5
listening **141**.35–6
as help for bereaved **116**.14–15
listeria **88**.28–9
literacy problems of employees **139**.17
litter **111**.3, 8–10, 19
bins **111**.9
campaigns **111**.8
as criminal offence **111**.19
legal definition **111**.9
liver cancer **60**.5, 9, 16, 17
liver damage and stem cell therapy **144**.22
living alone
lesbian, gay and bisexual people **101**.9
numbers of people **85**.2
single men **106**.12
living standards **98**.12
and water consumption **76**.8
living wills *see* advance directives (living wills)
Livingstone, Ken **115**.15
LL601 rice **138**.31–4
loans
student **139**.34
see also credit; debt
local authorities
duty to house **130**. 2–3
homelessness prevention funds **130**. 29–30
homelessness strategies **130**. 28
and litter **111**.8, 19
Local Authority care leavers, and homelessness **130**.11,
14
local communities **98**.38
and tourist development **109**.32
local economy, and tourism **109**.31
local government, women in **112**.18
Local Safeguarding Children Boards (LSCBs) **120**.15
London
affordable housing
and household growth **85**.29
and poverty **85**.10–12
supply and demand **85**.13
bombings
and faith hate crime **115**.27
impact on Muslims **115**.36
congestion charging **119**.12, 38
counter-terrorism measures in **92**.31–2
empty houses in **85**.13, 25
house prices **85**.3, 6
house-building in
brownfield versus greenfield debate **85**.16–17

numbers **85**.11
illegal radio stations **142**.7
multicultural tolerance **115**.23
overcrowding and poor housing conditions **85**.11–12
public opinion on housing **85**.13
religious diversity in **94**.6
lone parents **20**.26, 33; **124**.33–5; **133**.28–38
benefits available **133**.33–6
benefits claimed **133**.32, 36
children of **124**.22, 33–4; **133**.28, 31
and divorce **124**.33–4
and employment **133**.28
finding work **112**.12
help for **133**.37–8
and household income **133**.28, 30
and housing advice **133**.37
and poverty **110**.12–13, 17
statistics **106**.2, 3; **124**.35; **133**.28–32
teenage **126**.31; **133**.28
see also teenage pregnancies
loneliness
feelings after bereavement **116**.4, 19
and older people **105**.12
long-term poverty **110**.1, 6, 13
losing weight **113**.33
loss on childhood, and low self-esteem **117**.32
lotteries **129**.2
scams **134**.26
see also National Lottery
low carbon technologies **97**.4
low impact policing and football hooliganism **118**.8
low income families, holidays **110**.20
low self-esteem (LSE) **117**.5–8, 31
and bullying **122**.8
causes of **117**.31–2
and eating disorders **127**.2
and self-harm **136**.2
LPG vehicles **119**.20
LSD, mixed with other drugs **114**.16
lung cancer **145**.34
and cannabis use **128**.17, 19, 28

M

Macpherson Inquiry (Lawrence Report) **115**.8
macro-terrorism **92**.11
macrobiotic diet **140**.2
magazines
influence on body image **117**.11–12, 15
and sex education **142**.28, 29
magic mushrooms **114**.32, 35
magistrates court **137**.36
magnetic field therapy **81**.30, 31
Mailing Preference Service **134**.28
maintained schools, definition **135**.36
maintenance payments **133**.37
Make Poverty History coalition **110**.34
Making Good Progress consultation **139**.6
malaria **76**.6

and climate change **95**.7, 9, 12, 15, 17, 39
male stereotyping as barrier to university entrance **139**.38
malnutrition *see* hunger
managers
    management style and workplace bullying **122**.29, 35
    women **112**.18
    and workplace stress **100**.18, 25
mania **125**.19
manic depression *see* bipolar affective disorder
manufactured goods **98**.10
manufacturing sector employment **107**.7, 10
marijuana *see* herbal cannabis
marital status
    and population in England and Wales **106**.26
    and remarriages **106**.32
marker-assisted selection (MAS) **138**.37–9
marker genes **138**.4
market size, gambling industry **129**.4
    National Lottery **129**.9, 10
    online gambling **129**.17, 19
marketing alcohol to young people **143**.17
Marks & Spencer's
    and ethical trading **134**.30
    and Fairtrade **134**.36
marriage
    age at **106**.3, 25
    as an institution **106**.5–6
    as a relationship **106**.5–6
    arranged marriages **106**.15, 15–18; **108**.24
    attitudes to **106**.4–6, 11
    births outside **124**.22
    changing views on **106**.4–6, 20
    and Civil Partnerships **101**.33–4
    'common law' marriages **106**.8, 9–10
    early and forced marriage **120**.29
    forced marriages abroad **106**.15
    Government policies on **106**.31
    and HIV/AIDS **96**.24–5, 29, 34, 35
    inter-ethnic **115**.25
    and life expectancy **105**.30
    male and female attitudes to **106**.6
    open marriages **106**.18–19
    and premarital contracts **106**.22–4
    and rape **108**.6
    remarriages **106**.2, 3, 32
    statistics **106**.2, 3
    and stepfamilies *see* stepfamilies
    and tax incentives **106**.26
marriage counselling **106**.27
martyrdom, and suicide attacks **92**.16
Marxism, and terrorism **92**.7
masculinity **112**.33–4
    and gender equality **112**.36–8
    and health risks **112**.37
    rules of **112**.36
    and violence **112**.37–8
mass mourning **116**.17–18
massage **81**.4
    and raising self-esteem **117**.33
    see also aromatherapy

materials reclamation facility (MRF) **111**.3, 6
maternal mortality, global **112**.39
maternity leave **107**.16, 21
mathematics, A-level performance **139**.18
mature students **139**.30, 32
maximum working hours **107**.30–1
MDMA *see* ecstasy
means tested benefits **110**.18
meat consumption **88**.6, 26, 31; **140**.12–13, 15–18
    alternatives to meat **140**.19, 26
    effects **140**.13
    and fat **140**.12
    game as food source **140**.15, 17
    health issues **140**.13, 21, 30
    illegal meat **88**.39
    nutrients **140**.12, 14
meat-eaters, and opposition to animal experiments **103**.11
meat production
    effects of **140**.13, 16–17
    organic **140**.29–30
media
    accountability **142**.17–30
    and body image **117**.11–12, 15, 17–18; **127**.23
        and eating disorders **127**.25–6, 27
    breaking ethnic stereotypes **115**.22
    control **142**.1–16
    convergence **142**.1–2
    coverage of terrorism **92**.10, 23–4, 27, 28–9, 37
    and football-related violence **118**.7
    government control **121**.1
    government use of **121**.17–18
    and health care information **117**.18
    impact **142**.31–9
    intrusion **142**.23, 25, 26
    mergers **142**.4
    negative representation of young people **137**.24, 25
    ownership **121**.4–5
    and people with learning difficulties **135**.35
    portrayal of animal rights activists **103**.11
    portrayals of lesbians and gays **101**.15
    portrayal of disabled people **135**.29, 32
    and pressure on athletes to use drugs **118**.29
    and public perception of crime **137**.2
    and suicide **136**.37–9
    teenage magazines **142**.28
    violence *see* violence, media
    and women's sport **118**.21–2
    see also films; Internet; newspapers; radio; television
Media Watch **121**.36
mediation
    and divorce **106**.38–9
    and homelessness prevention **130**.30
medical abortion ('the abortion pill') **126**.10, 14, 32–4
medical benefits, GM crops **138**.9–10
    see also pharming
medical model of disability **135**.1
medical research and animal experimentation **140**.32–3; **144**.34
medical technology
    and advance directives **102**.36–7

and animal experiments **103**.10–11
and euthanasia **102**.1, 3, 29, 30, 31
medical treatment
and the mental capacity bill **102**.32
withdrawal of, and the law **102**.3
medical waste disposal **111**.36
medicinal use of cannabis **114**.39; **128**.4, 28, 36, 37
and the law **128**.37
multiple sclerosis **128**.36, 37
medicines
and alcohol **143**.10
animal testing of **103**.1, 11, 12–14
drug development **103**.2–3, 9, 10, 11, 13
and banned substances in sport **118**.32–3
from GM crops (pharming) **138**.4, 9–10, 20–22
and older people **105**.38–9
melanoma (skin cancer) **60**.5, 18, 19–21
memorial services **116**.17
memories of the deceased *see* remembrance of the
deceased
memory, effect of cannabis use **128**.4–5
men
and abortion
involvement in decision-making **126**.13, 15–16
rights **126**.15
and alcohol
alcohol consumption **143**.8, 31
safe limits **143**.26, 34
body image and the media **117**.12
and cancer **60**.3, 4, 5
breast cancer **60**.22
lung cancer **60**.4, 15, 26
prostate cancer **60**.3, 4, 6, 13, 24–5, 35
testicular cancer **60**.5, 18, 26
childcare careers **112**.23–4
and compulsive shopping **134**.14
and depression **125**.13–15
and divorce **106**.31
and eating disorders **127**.3
fertility and smoking **145**.32
and gender equality **112**.36–8
and gender identity **112**.36
and higher education **112**.1, 8
homosexual activity **133**.2
life expectancy **105**.2, 9, 19
lifestyle changes **112**.30
and mental ill-health **141**.1
older men and employment **105**.21, 22
and online shopping **134**.16
and self-harm **136**.2
and sexual health **96**.13
single **106**.3, 12, 20
and smoking **145**.21, 22
and stress **100**.13, 19
and suicide **136**.33, 35, 36
see also boys and young men; fathers; gay men;
infertility; masculinity
Men Into Childcare report **112**.23–4
meningitis **123**.5
menstruation, effect of overexercise **113**.23
mental health **141**.2, 34–6

and abortion **126**.11
and adolescents **123**.9
assessment after attempted suicide **136**.28
benefits of exercise **113**.22; **141**.34, 39
and cannabis **114**.37, 38; **128**.5, 8, 14–15
children **141**.37
and diet **125**.11–12; **141**.30–31, 34
and disability **135**.4
education in **141**.37
and homeless people **130**.11, 20, 27
and homophobia **101**.20
and older people **105**.3, 37–9
and smoking **145**.38–9
statistics **125**.16
and workplace stress **100**.17–18, 20
and youth crime **137**.13
see also dementia; depression
Mental Health Act 2007 **141**.26
mental illness
attitudes to **141**.25, 27
and cannabis **114**.37, 38
children **141**.1, 20–21
and criminal behaviour **141**.2, 22
definition **141**.1
and eating disorders **127**.9–10
genetic predisposition to **141**.24
help for people with **141**.34–6
and homelessness **130**.11, 20, 27
and medical research **103**.12
and poverty **141**.2, 22
prevalence **141**.1
see also depression; schizophrenia
mental impairment effects of ecstasy **114**.8
mental symptoms of workplace bullying **122**.31
mental toughness and resisting bullying **122**.38
mentoring **112**.16
mesomorph body shape **127**.22
metabolism **88**.15
effect of smoking **145**.26, 30–31
metals recycling **111**.23, 31, 36
aluminium **111**.11, 23–4, 26
methane
and global warming **95**.1, 4, 5, 6, 9
produced from landfill **111**.3, 15
Methodist Church **94**.1, 19
methyl alcohol (meths) **143**.1–2
Mexico, cannabis production **128**.24
Mexico City Policy (Global Gag Rule) **126**.19
mice
and creation of embryonic stem cells **144**.26
with human gene material **144**.11
microbes **88**.27, 28–9
microbicides **96**.34, 35
Microsoft
and Chinese censorship **121**.19
Workability initiative (disability) **135**.15
middle-classes
children as bullies **122**.9–10
cocaine use **114**.9
Mifepristone (the abortion pill) **126**.10, 14, 32–4
migrant worker exploitation **120**.30–31

migration **98**.2
    and climate change **95**.7, 12, 15, 17
    and population growth **20**.4–5, 6, 11
        in the UK **85**.29, 30
    see also asylum seekers; immigration
military personnel, suicides, Japan **136**.39
milk
    from cloned cows **144**.36–8, 39
    vegetarian alternatives **140**.22, 26
Millennialist faiths **94**.1, 2
Millennium Declaration **120**.3
Millennium Development Goals **110**.21, 23, 28, 29–31
    and child poverty **110**.35
millionaires, women **112**.19
minerals and vegetarian diets **140**.3
minicabs and disabled people **135**.9
minimum wage **107**.31
minority ethnic groups *see* ethnic minorities
miscegenation *see* mixed-race relationships
Misuse of Drugs Act 1971 (MDA) **114**.31–2, 33
mitochondrial DNA **144**.17
mixed-faith relationships **115**.39
mixed-race families **124**.36–7
mixed-race people, Britain **115**.24–5
    as victims of crime **115**.10
mixed-race relationships **115**.22–3, 24–5
MNCs (multi-national corporations) **98**.3, 25
mobile phones
    bullying by **122**.19, 21–5
    and the elderly **105**.10–11
    and gambling **129**.18, 26
    household ownership **134**.5
    and the Internet **104**.4–5
    and safety for children **104**.19
    tracking of **82**.19–20
    and young travellers **109**.13
mobility component, Disability Living Allowance **135**.5
mobius loop logo **111**.4
mock elections for young people **131**.27
models of disability **135**.1
moderate exercise **113**.25, 39
moderate poverty **110**.21
Modern Apprenticeships **107**.36
Mohammed, Danish cartoons of **121**.10–13, 15–16;
    142.34
money
    and the cashless society **74**.9–11
    and children **74**.4, 5–6, 6–7, 12–13
    financial abuse **105**.13; **108**.7, 15
    financial planning **74**.14–39
    management, regional differences **110**.15
    students **74**.1, 17, 19–22, 28–32, 34–9
    worries
    men **112**.30
    non-traditional families **124**.20
    young people **123**.3
    see also banks; credit; debt; incomes; wages
monoamine oxidase inhibitors (MAOIs) **125**.32
monogamy, and marriage **106**.18–19
Montessori method, encouraging children's
    independence **124**.13

mood
    and effects of alcohol **143**.7
    and effects of drugs **114**.2
mood stabilising drugs **125**.19, 25
Moonies **94**.19, 20
morbidity and coronary heart disease **113**.19
Mormons (Church of Jesus Christ of Latter-Day Saints)
    94.1, 19
morning after pill (emergency contraception) **126**.24
Morocco, cannabis production **128**.24
mortgages
    and first-time buyers **85**.6, 7
    help for lone parents **133**.34
    and interest rates **85**.6
    mortgage lending **134**.25
    and single people **85**.7
Moslems *see* Islam
mothers
    employment patterns **107**.26; **112**.12
    full-time **124**.12
    and poverty **110**.11, 17
    share of household tasks **124**.11
    single mothers and poverty **110**.17
    see also working mothers
motor neurone disease (MND) and stem cell research
    144.32–3
motoring
    costs **119**.14
    and disability **135**.7
    spending on **134**.4, 25
    trends **119**.7–9
    see also cars
motorways, active traffic management **119**.37
mourning *see* grief
mouth cancer **60**.5, 15
movie trafficking, and the Internet **104**.38–9
MPs and General Elections **131**.18
multiculturalism
    British Muslims support for **115**.34
    as hindrance to British identity **131**.10
    London **115**.23
multi-infarct dementia (vascular dementia) **105**.37; **141**.6
multinational companies, and tourism in developing
    countries **109**.19
multinational water corporations, and the privatisation
    of water supplies **76**.22, 23, 29–30
multiple identity concept of national identity **131**.10
multiple personality disorder **141**.12
multiple sclerosis (MS)
    and complementary medicine **81**.30–1
    and depression **125**.5
    and the medicinal use of cannabis **128**.36, 37
multiracial families **124**.36–7
multiracialism, Britain **115**.3, 23, 24–5, 38
multisensory alarms in cars **119**.19
mumps **123**.4–5
murder, bereavement by **116**.8
muscle dysmorphia **127**.19
muscle strength training **113**.23
muscular endurance **113**.24

music
  and mental health 141.36
  and raising self-esteem 117.33
Muslims
  British, feelings of identity 131.9
  fears after London bombings 115.36
  support for integration 115.34

N

nalbuphine hydrochloride 118.35
nalmefene 129.39
name changing, and children's rights 120.11
names for racial identity 115.4–5
nandrolone precursors 118.35
nappies, environmental impact 111.13–15
narcotic analgesics 118.38
nasal decongestants and ecstasy 114.16
National Anti-Doping Organisations (NADO) 118.26
National Association of Disabled Supporters (NADS) 118.22
National Black youth Forum 131.33–4
National Curriculum 139.1–2, 5–6
  and alcohol education 143.20
  pupils opinions 139.7
  and specialist diplomas 139.25
National Construction Week 112.25
national identity 131.1–14
  cards see identity cards
  effect of devolution 131.6
  and ethnic groups 131.8
  non-white ethnic groups 115.38
  register 120.35
National Institute for Clinical Excellence (NICE) 127.28, 29
National Lottery 129.9–13
  good causes 129.9
  Olympic Games funding 129.9
  online, and under 16s 129.12–13
  and under 16s 129.11–13
national origin as grounds for discrimination 115.7
National Playing Fields Association 118.5, 6
National Registered Testing Pool (NRTP) 118.31
National Healthy Schools Programme 123.31
National Viewers' and Listeners' Association 121.36
National Workplace Bullying Survey 122.33
nationalist terrorism 92.2, 7
nationality as grounds for discrimination 115.7
natural burial 134.31
natural cloning 144.1
Natural Death Centre 116.39
natural gas vehicles 119.20–21
natural medicine see complementary medicine (CM)
natural resources 98.21; 111.4
  and poverty reduction 110.25–6
nature and mental wellbeing 117.38–9
naturopathy 81.2, 19
NCH and mobile phone bullying 122.22–4, 25
needs, children 120.2
negative body image see body image, negative

negative discipline 132.18
negative experiences, learning from 117.6
negative representation of young people 137.24, 25
negative thinking and low self-esteem 117.6
neglect
  children 132.1–2, 4–5
  and older people 105.13
nervous system diseases and depression 125.5
Netherlands, The
  Beyond Compare Photo Tour 117.13
  cannabis availability 128.28
  extremist parties 131.23
neurobiology and gambling 129.6
neuroblastoma in children 60.9, 10
neurosis 141.1
neurotransmitters 141.9
New Deal for Lone Parents (NDLP) 112.12
news
  attitudes to 142.31–3
  being interviewed 142.11–12
  effect of media ownership 142.5
  sources 142.33
News Corporation 121.5
news manipulation 121.6
newspapers 142.8–9
  advertising 134.8
  cartoons of Mohammed 121.10–13, 15–16; 142.34
  and Freedom of Information Act 142.17
  mergers 142.4
  ownership 121.4–5
  readership 142.8
  sales 142.9
  as source of news 142.33
NGOs (non-governmental organisations), and global water supplies 76.30, 31
NHS (National Health Service) 108.10
  and abortion 126.12, 24
  and cancer treatment 60.6
  and complementary medicine 60.39; 81.4, 21
    costs of 81.31
    effectiveness of 81.22
    funding 81.27, 29, 36
    and multiple sclerosis 81.30–1
    osteopathy 81.7
    reflexology 81.17, 31
    support for 81.30–1
  and eating disorders 127.28
  and HIV treatments 96.21, 22
NHS Direct 126.7
nicotine 114.5
  addiction 145.25–7, 35
  chemical content 145.25
  children 145.2–3
  effects on the body 145.25–6
  gum 145.37
  inhalator 145.37
  nasal spray 145.37
  patches 145.37
    and young people 145.20
  replacement therapy 145.33, 37
  toxicity 145.27

withdrawal symptoms **145**.26–7
night eating syndrome **127**.17–18
night shelters **130**.31
nitrogen oxide (NOx) emissions, transport **119**.15, 16
nitrous oxide, and global warming **95**.1, 4, 6, 9
no-blame policy and bullying **122**.12
no-torture agreements and deportation **120**.38
non-contributory benefits **110**.18
Non-Hodgkin's lymphoma **60**.4, 9, 10
non-maintained special schools **135**.36
non-means tested benefits **110**.18
non-renewable resources **111**.4
non-reproductive cloning *see* therapeutic cloning
non-traditional families **124**.20–21
non-traditional jobs for women **112**.21, 25–7
non-violent direct action **121**.14
North-South divide **110**.15
Northern Ireland *see* Ireland, Northern
nose operations, and self-esteem **117**.27
Not Seen, not Heard report **135**.35
NRMs (New Religious Movements) **94**.19–25
    and anti-cult movements **94**.21
    and anti-discrimination legislation **94**.35, 36
    changes in **94**.19–20
    characteristics associated with **94**.19
    cults and mind control **94**.22–3
    cults recruiting from universities **94**.24–5
    dangers associated with **94**.20–1
    defining **94**.19
    diversity among **94**.19
    joining **94**.20–2
    members in the UK **94**.21
NSPCC *Be the FULL STOP* campaign **132**.5–6
Nubain **118**.35
nuclear power **95**.5, 34; **97**.3–4, 19–23
    building new power stations **97**.21–2
    and clean-up of nuclear weapons material **97**.23
    and climate change **97**.19–20, 21, 22
    costs of **97**.6
    debate over **97**.7
    disadvantages of **97**.2, 7, 8
    and electricity generation **97**.3–4, 22–3
    environmental issues surrounding **97**.2, 4
    and nuclear waste **97**.20, 22, 23
    and radioactive discharges **97**.20
    and renewable energy **97**.6, 7, 19, 21
    and terrorism **97**.20
numbness
    and traumatic bereavement **116**.10
    see also shock
numeracy problems, employees **139**.17
nutrition
    and meat **140**.12, 14
    and mental health **141**.30–31, 34
    teenagers **123**.6–7
    vegetarians **140**.3–4, 6, 11
    see also diet; healthy eating
nutritional supplements **118**.28
    and anti-doping rules **118**.33
NVQs (National Vocational Qualifications) **139**.4

obesity **88**.4, 9–11; **113**.1–5, 6, 7–12, 15; **127**.32–9
    avoidance *see* weight management
    and Body Mass Index (BMI) **113**.9, 11
    in children *see* childhood obesity
    and coronary heart disease **113**.20
    defining **113**.9, 11; **127**.33
    economic costs **88**.4; **127**.33–4, 37
    and employment **113**.17, 18
    and genetics **127**.35
    and health **113**.5, 7, 10; **127**.32, 34
    and life expectancy **105**.30
    measurement **113**.7, 9, 11, 15
        children **127**. 36, 37
    risk groups **113**.9–10
    statistics **113**.2, 9–10, 11–12; **127**.32, 33, 34
        children **113**.3, 12
    treatment strategies **113**.12
        see also weight management
    and worker productivity **113**.18
    and young people **123**.31
    see also body weight
Obesity Taskforce, International **113**.12
obestatin (appetite-suppressing hormone) **127**.38–9
obsessions **141**.17
obsessive compulsive disorder (OCD) **141**.17
occupational choice, non-traditional
    men **112**.23–4
    women **112**.21, 25–7
oesophageal cancer **60**.4, 15, 17
Ofcom **121**.36
    and illegal broadcasting **142**.7
    and media mergers **142**. 4
offences, drug misuse **114**.31
Offences against the Person Act **126**.7
offender management bill **137**.30
offender release, victim's rights **137**.28
Offending, Crime and Justice survey **137**.16–17
offending and mental health problems **125**.16
offensive language, television **121**.38–9
Office for Disability Issues **135**.23–4
offices, waste prevention **111**.16
Official Secrets **121**.1–2
offshore wind farms **97**.12, 16, 26
oil
    depletion of resources **97**.8, 10
    leakages **97**.3
    oil production and climate change **95**.16–17
    recycling **111**.24, 35
    and renewable energy **97**.10
older people
    in care homes **105**.15
    and depression **125**.22–3
    excessive drinking **143**.9–10, 30
    and health **105**.3, 5, 28–39
    and homelessness **130**.17–18
    and mental health problems **125**.16; **141**.2
    and money matters **105**.34
    poverty **110**.19–20

women **112**.20
  at risk of abuse **105**.13–14
  and self-harm **136**.20
  statistics **105**.4–6
older workers **105**.16–27; **107**.12–13
  and flexible working **105**.19–20, 27
  and legislation on age discrimination **105**.18, 20,
    23–4, 26
  women **105**.21–2
Olympic Games
  drug testing **118**.25
  National Lottery funding **129**.9
omega 3 fatty acids
  and attention-deficit hyperactivity disorder **141**.19
  in eggs **140**.39
  in meat **140**.12, 21
one-parent families *see* lone parents
online brands **142**.35
online bullying **122**.19–26
online child abuse **132**.33
  images **132**.31–2
online dating scams **134**.27
online fraud **134**.26–9
online gambling **129**.17–18, 19–25
  and addiction **129**.21–2
  Europe **129**.20
  National Lottery games and under 16s **129**.12–13
  participation rates **129**.17, 19
  poker, underage **129**.25
  at work **129**.22–4
online grooming **132**.33
online journalism register **142**.16
online learning **139**.28
online reporting of crime **137**.31
online retail *see* Internet shopping
onlineaholism **142**.37
open marriages **106**.18–19
Open University **139**.28
Orange, workplace travel plan **119**.33
organ donation **116**.31
organ transplants *see* therapeutic cloning
organic farming
  animal welfare **140**.35–6
  meat production **140**.29–30
  unable to meet demand for food **140**.36–7
organic food **88**.13–14, 18, 33, 34
  and Fairtrade **134**.37
organic shops **134**.30, 31
organic waste **111**.4, 23
  composting **111**.6, 23, 31, 33
organized crime bill **137**.30
Orthodox Churches **94**.1, 2
orthorexia nervosa **127**.19
Orwell, George, and censorship **121**.7
osteopathy **81**.6–7, 23, 36
osteoporosis **105**.3, 32
  and chiropractic **81**.9
ostrich farming **140**.30
Ouseley, Lord Herman **115**.33
out-of-school learning **139**.27–8
outdoor activities and mental well-being **117**.38–9

outdoor (released) GMOs **138**.12
outreach teams for homeless people **130**.31
overdoses *see* drug overdoses
overdrafts **134**.22, 24
  regional differences **110**.15
overexercise **113**.23, 27–8, 27–8
overgeneralisation and low self-esteem **117**.6
overseas students **139**.30, 31, 32
overseas travel trends **119**.1
overweight people **127**.32, 33
  children **119**.31
  and coronary heart disease **113**.20
  health of **113**.16
  see also obesity
ownership of the media **121**.4–5
  effect on news **142**.5
  mergers **142**.4
  newspapers **142**.9
Oxfam and gender equality **112**.39

P

Pack-Flow project **111**.25
packaging
  food **111**.11
  waste **111**.5, 10, 22
Packaging Waste Directive **111**.2, 10
paedophiles **132**.22
  help for **132**.36–9
  and homosexuality **101**.17
  see also child pornography; sex offenders
paedophobia (fear of young people) **137**.26–7
Paganism **94**.2
pain
  absence during self-harm **136**.
  and exercise **113**.28
pain relief
  and acupuncture **81**.5
  and euthanasia **102**.29, 31
  right to **102**.4–5
pain response, gender differences **112**.32
paint recycling **111**.35
Pakistani pupils and education **115**.18
Palestinian terrorist groups
  first-century **92**.1
  Hamas **92**.2, 20, 21
  and suicide attacks **92**.15–16
palliative care
  and death with dignity **102**.30
  and terminal illnesses **102**.9, 12–13
pancreas repair, stem cell therapy **144**.21
pancreatic cancer **60**.4, 16, 17
panic attacks after bereavement **116**.4
paper
  packaging waste **111**.11
  recycling **111**.24, 27, 31, 32, 36
Paraguay, cannabis production **128**.24
Paralympic Games, National Lottery funding **129**.9
paranoia **141**.5

parasuicide **123**.36; **136**.24
Parental Guidance (PG) classification **121**.29
parental leave **107**.21
parental responsibility **124**.4; **133**.39
parenting **124**.1–19
    styles **124**.8
Parenting Orders **137**.12
Parentline Plus **124**.16–17
    and bullying **122**.15–16
    and stepfamilies **124**.28
parents
    absence due to divorce, effect on children **124**.34
    and adult children **124**.3, 14–15
    and the age of consent **101**.27
    and alcohol
        alcohol abuse **143**.37
        influence on young people **143**.5, 17
    authoritarian **124**.8
    authoritative **124**.8
    awareness of mobile bullying **122**.25
    of bisexuals **101**.17
    of bullies **122**.8–9
    celebrity role models **124**.6
    and child labour **99**.3
    and children as consumers **134**.12
    and children's diet **113**.4, 8
    and children's gender development **112**.35
    and children's participation **120**.10
    and children's television viewing **121**.26, 27, 32
    and children's video game use **121**.32–3
    cohabiting and married **106**.21–2
    death of **116**.12–13
    disciplining children **132**.18
    discussing eating disorders **127**.25
    divorcing **106**.33–8
    of drug users **114**.24
    employment, and child poverty **110**.12
    and exam stress **123**.30
    fathers' rights and responsibilities
    fears over child safety **124**.13–14
    feelings of failure **124**.16–17
    homosexuality and the repeal of section 28 **101**.18
    and the Internet
        and online learning **104**.9–10
        and online safety **104**.19, 20–1
        skills gap between parents and children **104**.4
    of lesbians and gays
        and choice **101**.15–16
        coming out to **101**.2–3, 11, 12, 13
        and emotions **101**.16–17
        and fear of rejection **101**.15
        organisations for **101**.16
        reactions of parents **101**.15
        and upbringing **101**.5, 16
    with mental health problems **141**.24–5
    and mobile phone tracking **82**.20
    and money matters
        savings **74**.7
        teaching children about **74**.1, 5–6
    non-traditional families **124**.20–21
    and obesity in children **113**.3

parenting skills **124**.2
parenting styles **124**.8; **132**.18
    permissive **124**.8
    and pregnant teenagers **126**.28, 29
    protection of children **137**.20
    and RE (religious education) **94**.15
    responsibilities **124**.4, 5; **133**.39
    rights **133**.39
    same-sex partnerships and the right to parenthood
        101.9, 31
    and self-harm by children **136**.14
    sex education involvement **133**.12, 15
    and smacking **132**.8–11, 15–16, 17
    smoking, effects on children **145**.2, 32–3
    and stress **100**.13
    and student finance **74**.19, 38; **139**.34, 35
    support for **120**.13; **124**.5, 6, 16–17
    supporting adult children **124**.3
    of teenagers **124**.16–17
    time spent with children **106**.2
    unmarried **124**.22
    weight, and children's obesity **113**.3
    see also birth parents; divorce; families; fathers; lone
        parents; mothers; working parents
parking
    concessions for disabled people **135**.7–8
    illegal **119**.9
Parkinson's disease
    and dementia **141**.6
    and depression **125**.5
    and ecstasy **114**.4
Parliament **131**.15
    women in **112**.18
part-time jobs **107**.17, 18, 19, 22
    children and teenagers with **74**.6, 8, 9
    and older people **105**.20
    and the pay gap **112**.17
    and students **74**.20, 37; **139**.35
participation rights, children **120**.9–11
participation in sport **118**.9
    adults **118**.1
    female **118**.18–20
    school team sports **118**.4
    young people **118**.2; **123**.2
        long term benefits **137**.26
particulates emissions **119**.15
parties and alcohol **123**.17
parties, political *see* political parties
passive euthanasia, religious views on **102**.2, 12
passive smoking **145**.2, 28–9
    effect on children **123**.12; **145**.2, 28–9
passports **89**.33
    and identity cards **82**.9–10, 12
passwords
    and children **104**.27
    and e-shopping **104**.6
    and pharming **104**.34
pastoral care in schools and gender equality **112**.9–10
patents **138**.4
    genes **138**.23
paternity leave **107**.21

pathological gambling *see* compulsive gambling
Patient Advice and Liaison Services (PALS) **127**.29
patient confidentiality *see* confidentiality
pay gap **112**.16–17, 20
PE in schools **118**.3
PE School Sport and Club Links (PESSCL) **118**.3
peaceful protesting **121**.14
pedestrians and road accidents **119**.5, 30–31
peer pressure
    on athletes to use drugs **118**.29
    and children's food choices **123**.32
    and drinking behaviour **143**.17
    and drug use **128**.10
    and sexual intercourse **123**.21
    and smoking **145**.4
peer support
and bullying **122**.12
and self-harm **136**.8, 16, 18
PEGI game classification system **121**.33
penal system, prohibition of corporal punishment **132**.15
penalties
    cannabis cultivation **128**.31
    cannabis supply **128**.2, 9, 13
    drink-driving **143**.24
    for drug smuggling **114**.35
    for littering **111**.19
    and Misuse of Drugs Act **114**.32
    possession of drugs **114**.36
      cannabis **128**.2, 9, 13, 27, 30, 31, 32
    underage sale of alcohol **143**.2
pensions **89**.23; **110**.19, 20
    and the longevity revolution **105**.36
    pension crisis **105**.19, 25, 26
    and same-sex partnerships **101**.30, 34
    saving for **134**.4, 25
      graduates **139**.36
    state pensions **105**.5, 19, 25
    and women **112**.20
    and young people **74**.1–2
Pentecostalism **94**.2
People in Harmony (organisation for mixed-race
    families) **124**.37
peptide hormones and analogues **118**.37
periods, effect of overexercise **113**.23
permafrost, and climate change **95**.15, 19, 24
permissive parenting style **124**.8
persistent poverty **110**.6, 13
personal crime, racial identity of victims **115**.10
personality and depression susceptibility **125**.2
pesco-vegetarian diet **140**.2
pester power **134**.12
pesticides **88**.13, 32, 34, 35
    GM viruses **138**.13–14
petrol prices **119**.12–13, 14
    see also fuel taxes
pets, death of **116**.13–14
Pfizer, workplace travel plan **119**.33
pharmaceutical industry
    and animal experiments **103**.9, 12–14
    and herbal medicine **81**.11
pharming **104**.33–4

Phillips, Trevor **115**.6, 22, 28–9
phishing **104**.32–3; **134**.27–8, 28–9
PESSCL (PE School Sport and Club Links) **118**.3
PG film classification **121**.29
pharming **138**.4, 9–10, 20–22
    hens for cancer treatment **138**.20–21
    rice **138**.20
    risks **138**.20, 21, 22
    tobacco plants for HIV treatment **138**.21–2
phobias **141**.16–17
    and young people **100**.2
phone bothering by parents **124**.15
phone-tapping in the workplace **120**.33
physical abuse **108**.5, 19
    of children **132**.1, 4
    effect on children **108**.19
    and older people **105**.13
    signs of **132**.4
    and stress **100**.1, 2
physical activity *see* exercise
physical addiction to drugs **114**.17–18
physical characteristics, influence on drug effects **114**.2
physical punishment *see* corporal punishment
physical signs of bullying **122**.13, 30, 31
physician-assisted suicide (PAS) **102**.4, 7, 9
    arguments against **102**.23
    arguments for **102**.22–3
    defining **102**.22
    and euthanasia **102**.22
    and the law **102**.15, 21, 23
    and the medical profession **102**.20–1, 23, 27
    statistics **102**.17
    see also assisted suicide
phytochemicals **88**.5, 7, 13
pica **127**.17
Pick's disease **141**.7
pigeons, feeding on waste **111**.12–13
pill, contraceptive **123**.23
    risk alert, impact on teenage pregnancy rate **126**.31
pirate radio **142**.7
PISA (Programme for International Student
    Achievement) **139**.2
placebo effect, and complementary medicine **81**.26, 28,
    34
planning applications and sports facilities **118**.5
plants
    and climate change **95**.3, 9, 11, 14–15
    endangered species **78**.2–3, 7
    and photosynthesis **97**.9
    in tropical rainforests **78**.11
    see also genetically modified (GM) crops
plasmids **138**.2
plastic bottles recycling **111**.26–7
plastic surgery *see* cosmetic surgery
plastic waste **111**.2, 12, 23
    and energy production **111**.2
    recycling 26–7, 31, 36
playground bullying and screen violence **121**.28
playing fields **118**.5–6
plumbing as career for women **112**.26
pneumonia **105**.2

pocket money **74**.6, 8, 9, 13, 14
poisoning, first aid **136**.23
poker, online, and underage gambling **129**.25
police **137**.32–4
    arrest, your rights **128**.35–6
    and asylum communities **89**.20
    and beggars **130**.33
    and child abuse **132**.3
    and child protection on the Internet **104**.28–9
    Community Support Officers (CSO) **137**.33
    and counter-terrorism **92**.33, 34, 38
        and the Muslim community **92**.28, 29
    and drugs offences **114**.36
    and football hooliganism **118**.8
    and identity cards **82**.8
    and instant justice **137**.34
    and the law on hunting **103**.31
    and online child pornography **99**.24
    and racial discrimination **137**.32–3
    recorded crime figures **137**.3
    reporting abuse to **108**.10; 3
    reporting a crime to **137**.30
    and surveillance **82**.23
    women in police force **112**.18
    young people's opinions of **137**.14
policy-making and Convention on the Rights of the
    Child **120**.6
political action and eating disorders **127**.26
political parties **131**.18
    young peoples's support **131**.32
political pressure on athletes **118**.29
politics
    and competitive sport **118**.4
    and crime **137**.1–2
    and free speech **121**.7
    and genomics **138**.3
    and the media **142**.2
    and newspapers **142**.8
    recommendations for change **131**.25
    and support of media companies **121**.5
    women in **112**.18, 39
    young people's involvement **131**.27–35
    see also elections
portage educational support **135**.36
postal voting **131**.16
pollution
    from aviation **119**.16
    and endangered species **78**.6
        in the UK **78**.28, 29, 32
    paper mills **111**.32
    and population growth **20**.14, 23, 24
    and species extinction **78**.11
    and transport **119**.12, 13–14, 16, 30, 31
        see also emissions, transport
    see also air pollution; water pollution
polydrug use **114**.2, 16–17
poppers
    and the law **114**.32
    and viagra **114**.16
population changes
    see ageing population; population growth

population density and refugees **89**.23
population growth **20**.1–40; **89**.31
    and AIDS **20**.3, 5, 7, 11
    and endangered species **78**.1
    and global warming **95**.9
    and global water shortages **76**.3, 5, 8, 15
    and immigration **20**.4–5, 11, 15–16, 32
    and migration **85**.29, 30
    and population density **20**.2
    rates of **20**.1, 4, 7, 10, 20, 25, 26, 33, 36
    and water consumption **76**.22, 29
population migration **98**.2
population studies (epidemology) **103**.17, 18, 19, 22
pornography
    and the Internet
        arrests and convictions **104**.29
        and children and young people **104**.4, 18, 23, 24,
            25, 26–7
        R18 films **121**.25, 20
    see also child pornography
Portman Group **143**.27
positive action and sex discrimination **112**.14
positive body image **117**.10
positive discipline **132**.18
Positive Image campaign **112**.25
positive sex discrimination **112**.14
positive thinking **117**.2, 6; **141**.36
    as help for depression **125**.3
possession of drugs **114**.36
    cannabis **128**.2, 9, 13, 27, 30, 31, 32
post-compulsory education **139**.2
    see also higher education; universities
post-mortem examination **116**.32
post-natal depression **125**.4, 17–18
    diagnosis of **125**.17
    symptoms of **125**.17
    treatment for **125**.17–18
post-traumatic stress disorder (PTSD) **108**.2; **116**.10;
    137.29; **141**.3, 12
potatoes, GM research trials **138**.27, 28
poverty **98**.5–6, 18
    and affordable housing
        in rural areas **85**.5
    causes of **110**.22
    and child labour **99**.2, 3, 4, 14–15; **120**.19
    and child protection abuses **110**.39
    children living in **106**.3
    defining and measuring **110**.1, 21, 22, 29
    and disabled people **135**.16–18
    and elderly people **110**.19–20
    global **110**.21–39
    and global warming **95**.9, 35
    and globalisation **98**.1, 13, 35–6
    and health **110**.35
    and HIV/AIDS **96**.24, 29
    incomes **98**.5, 13, 18, 32, 33
    and international trade **98**.9, 14, 15, 21
    measuring **110**.1, 29
    and mental health problems **141**.2, 22
    and Millennium Development Goals **110**.29–30
    effect on mothers and babies **110**.11

older people living in **105**.4–5, 25
and population growth **20**.9, 33
and post traumatic stress disorder **141**.3
public opinions **110**.34
reduction **110**.23
  and natural resources **110**.25–6
  statistics **110**.29
  targets **110**.6–7, 21, 23, 28, 29–31
of the rich **110**.22–3
rich-poor gap **98**.33–4
and segregation **115**.30, 31, 32
and the sexual exploitation of children **99**.16, 24
and smoking **145**.21
statistics **110**.2, 21, 23, 29
  global **110**.35, 36
  UK **110**.2, 7
and teenage pregnancy **133**.20, 21
in the UK **110**.1–20
and water
  and development aid **76**.30–1
  and human rights **76**.25
  multinational water corporations **76**.29
  supplies in developing countries **76**.6
and women **110**.11, 17–18, 19, 22
see also child poverty; inequality
poverty line **110**.1, 12, 22
power and self-esteem **117**.4, 31–2
Power to the People report **131**.25
Prader-Willi Syndrome **127**.17
praise and self-esteem **117**.34
pre-implantation genetic diagnosis **144**.20
pre-school children
  effects of divorce **124**.33
  normal sexual behaviour **132**.29–30
precursor cells **144**.25
pregnancy
  and alcohol **143**.3, 25, 27, 33–4
  development **126**.26
  and HIV **96**.16, 22, 23, 31, 38
  and male depression **125**.14
  men's rights **126**.15
  planned, teenagers **133**.20
  and poverty **110**.11
  and smoking **88**.7; **145**.32–3
  testing **133**.8
  unplanned, options **126**.9–10
see also abortion; teenage pregnancies
Pregnancy Advisory Service, British (BPAS) **126**.7
prejudice
  definition **115**.4
  in childhood, and low self-esteem **117**.32
  against disabled people **135**.15, 30–31
  and homophobic bullying **101**.3
  Islamaphobia **115**.36
  racial **131**.2
  religious **131**.3
see also discrimination
premature deaths from coronary heart disease **113**.19
prenuptial contracts **106**.22–4
press *see* media
Press Code **142**.26

Press Complaints Commission **142**.26, 30
  and suicide reporting **142**.30
press conferences **142**.12–13
pressure on athletes to use drugs **118**.29
prices
  alcohol, effect on consumption **143**.17, 31
  cigarettes **145**.17
    as deterrent to children smoking **145**.3
  drugs **114**.6–7
    falling **114**.9, 22
    cannabis **128**.2, 6
Primark and ethical trading **134**.30
primary age children, effects of divorce **124**.33
primary schools
  curriculum **139**.5, 6
  gender gap **112**.8
  pupil behaviour **120**.16
  and pupils' mental health **141**.37
see also schools
primate with jelly fish genes **144**.11
prisons **137**.37–9
  and children **120**.12
  corporal punishment prohibition **132**.15
  costs **137**.37
  prison leavers and homelessness **130**.11, 15
  prison population **137**.1, 37
    international comparisons **137**.38
  Prison Rules **137**.38
  prisoners' rights **137**.37–8
  private prisons **137**.2
  and self-harm **137**.37
  sentences for cannabis possession **128**.13
  and women **137**.39
see also youth custody
privacy
  children's right to **120**.12
  and the media **142**.25, 26
see also freedom of information
privacy enhancing technology (PET), and RFID tags
    82.16
privacy rights **82**.1–3, 39
  bodily privacy **82**.5
  and communications data **82**.1–2
  communications privacy **82**.5
  comprehensive laws on **82**.5
  defining privacy **82**.4
  and human rights **82**.4–5, 18
  information privacy **82**.5
  models of privacy protection **82**.5
  and RFID tags **82**.13–17, 35
  and technologies of privacy **82**.5
  viewpoints on privacy **82**.4
  in the workplace **82**.25–30
private communication interception **120**.34
private sales and consumer rights **134**.20
privatisation
  impact on poverty **110**.22
  and water management **76**.22–3, 32
    criticisms of private companies **76**.32
    multinational water corporations **76**.22, 23,
    29–30

pro-abortion arguments **126**.21
pro-life arguments **126**.21–2
pro-life movement **126**.25
  and abortion time-limit **126**.38
pro-poor tourism **109**.27, 38
problem debt **134**.23
problem drinking *see* alcohol abuse
problem gambling *see* compulsive gambling
Producer Responsibility Obligations (packaging waste)
    Regulations **111**.10
Programme for International Student Achievement
    (PISA) **139**.2
Prohibited Substances and Methods, List of **118**.27, 31
promoters, sports, pressure on athletes to use drugs
    118.29
prosecutions for littering **111**.9
prostate cancer **60**.3, 4, 6, 24–5; **105**.10
prostitution and child sex tourism **109**.35
protection of children
    from abuse **120**.14–15
    refugees **120**.22
protectionism **98**.9, 10–11, 24
protectiveness, parental **124**.13–14
proteins **88**.6, 8
    definition **138**.4
    drugs produced by GM hens **138**.20–21
    and vegan diet **140**.23–4
    and vegetarian diet **140**.3, 7
Protestant traditions and beliefs **94**.1, 2
PSHE (personal, social and health education) **133**.16
psilocin **114**.35
psilocybin **114**.35
psoriasis and smoking **145**.30
psychiatric patients and smoking **145**.38
psychic prediction scams **134**.26
psychological abuse
    and older people **105**.13
psychological addiction to drugs **114**.18
psychological bullying **122**.10
psychological conditions and eating disorders **127**.9–10
psychological damage caused by corporal punishment
    132.10
psychological dependency on cannabis **128**.8
psychological distress caused by obesity **113**.7
psychological effects of nicotine **145**.26
psychological health requirements **117**.8
psychologists, and young people and stress **100**.2
psychology and gambling **129**.6, 29
psychosis **141**.1
    cannabis use **128**.15
psychosurgery **125**.26
psychotherapy
    and bipolar disorder **141**.14–15
    as a treatment for depression **125**.7, 26, 33
    and young people and stress **100**.2
PTSD (post-traumatic stress disorder) **108**.2; **116**.10;
    137.29; **141**.3, 12
puberty **127**.22
    and eating disorders **127**.2, 22–4

public attitudes
    to biotechnology **138**.15–16; **144**.19
    to cannabis use **128**.12
    to film classification **121**.24
    to genetic modification **138**.3; **144**.20
    to healthy eating campaigns **113**.13
    to human cloning **144**.35
    to Internet use **104**.15
    to marriage and cohabitation **106**.4–6
    to mental ill-health **141**.25, 27
    to refugees **89**.17
    to smacking **132**.8, 18
    to smoking ban **145**.18
    to world poverty **110**.34
public appointments, women **112**.18
public grief **116**.17–18
public interest
    and journalists' rights **142**.27
    and media mergers **142**.4
Public Order Act **143**.2
public policing, littering **111**.8
public safety and censorship **121**.13
public service broadcasting, news coverage **142**.33
public transport **119**.1, 12, 25
    and disabled people **135**.8
    encouraging use of **119**.39
pubs
    and smoking ban **145**.13
    and young people **143**.2
punishment
    in schools, and racism **115**.19
    see also penalties
pupils
    behaviour **120**.16
    opinions on National Curriculum **139**.7
pupil referral units **135**.36
Putting U in the picture campaign **122**.22–3, 25
Puttnam, Lord David **121**.28
pyramid selling **134**.26

Q

Quakers (Religious Society of Friends) **94**.2
qualifications **89**.34–5; **107**.1, 34; **139**.4
    and ethnicity **139**.8
    and gender **112**.1, 8; **139**.10
    for university entrance **139**.29–30
    see also A-levels; AS-levels; degrees; educational
        achievement; GCSEs
quality of goods, consumer rights **134**.2, 17
quality of life, and euthanasia **102**.2, 29, 30
quitting smoking *see* smoking, giving up
Quorn **140**.19
quotations and consumer rights **134**.18
Qu'ran (Koran) **94**.2, 10
    and terrorism **92**.26, 29, 37

R

R18 film classification **121**.25, 30
rabbit-human embryos **144**.11
race
 definition **115**.4
 as grounds for discrimination **115**.7
 names for **115**.4–5
race hate trials **121**.15
Race Relations Act **115**.2, 7–8
 and bullying **122**.4, 11
racial background, UK population **115**.3, 24–5
racial discrimination **115**.4, 7–8
 and academic freedom **121**.8, 9
 in employment **115**.13
 see also racism
racial equality in football **118**.15–16
racial harassment
 defining **115**.8
 of refugees **89**.19, 20
racial identity, victims of crime **115**.10
racial integration **107**.12; **115**.6, 28–9; **131**.9
 Asians **115**.37
 in education **115**.29, 33
Racial and Religious Hatred Bill **121**.7, 15
racial segregation **115**.28–32
racially motivated crime **115**.9–10
racism **115**.1–2, 4
 challenging **115**.2
 and ChildLine **115**.1
 and children **115**.9
 defining **115**.4
 and education **115**.19–20
 effects of **115**.1
 in football **118**.14
 and Islamophobia **94**.34–5; **115**.36
 laws **115**.2, 7–8, 11–12, 26
 perception of **131**.2
 and the police **137**.32–3
 reasons for **115**.1–2
 in schools **115**.9, 19–20; **139**.9
 in the workplace **115**.11–14
 see also discrimination; employment and racism;
  ethnic minorities; racial discrimination
racist bullying **115**.2; **122**.4–5
racist incidents **115**.9
racist violence **137**.8, 16
radio
 interviews **142**.13–14
 as news source **142**.33
 pirate stations **142**.7
railways
 congestion **119**.35
 and disabled people **135**.8
 travel trends **119**.1
rainfall
 and climate change **95**.2–3, 7, 14, 16
 and water distribution in the UK **76**.1–2
rainforests *see* forestry
random drug tests in schools **114**.26

rape
 marital rape **108**.6
 number of reported rapes **137**.8
 statutory **101**.27
 and women's economic autonomy **112**.38
Rastafarians **94**.2
rate of return on education **139**.1, 37
RE (religious education) **94**.9–10, 15, 31, 37
re-offending rates, young offenders **137**.11, 15
reactive depression **125**.4
Real Parents campaign **124**.6
reality TV
 breaking ethnic stereotypes **115**.22
 and offensive language **121**.38–9
reclassification of cannabis **128**.13, 26–8, 29
 criticized **128**.38
 effect on health **128**.30–32, 38
 public attitudes to **128**.12
recombinant DNA technologies *see* genetic
  modification
recruitment of employees, discrimination **115**.13
recycling **111**.4, 15, 17, 22–37
 aluminium **111**.11, 23–4, 26
 campaigns **111**.25
 cans **111**.11, 23, 26
 collections **111**.3, 29
 glass **111**.11, 23, 27, 28, 31, 36
 household waste **111**.6
 incentives **111**.34, 37
 oil **111**.24, 35
 organic waste *see* composting waste
 paper **111**.24, 27, 31, 32, 36
 plastic **111**.26–7, 31, 36
 targets **111**.37
Red Cross Escort service **135**.9
redress (compensation) **134**.2, 17
reduce, reuse, recycle **111**.1, 3
reducing waste **111**.4, 17
 businesses **111**.18
reflexology **81**.3, 15–17, 23, 36
 and stress-related illnesses **81**.16
 training as a reflexologist **81**.16–17
refugees **120**.31
 children **120**.21–2
 and climate change **95**.12, 15, 17
 and homelessness **130**.11–12, 19
 and population growth **20**.11
 see also asylum seekers
refuges **108**.21, 32–3, 34–5, 37
regional differences
 child poverty **110**.13
 childhood obesity **113**.3
 disability **135**.2
 money management **110**.15
 smoking **145**.1, 21
register of GM land, proposals for **138**.19, 36
registering a death **116**.31
regulation
 of children's viewing **121**.26–7
 of cloning **144**.3
 of genetic modification **138**.3, 11

film 121.22–5, 29–30
of hybrid embryo research 144.14
media
and civil liberties 142.1–2
mergers 142.4
online journalism 142.16
stem cell cloning 144.27–8
television 121.36–7
video 121.26, 31
video games 121.32–3
Regulation of Investigatory Powers Act (RIP) 120.32
relationship support 106.29–30
relationships
and boys' culture 112.34
breakdown, and homelessness 130.3, 11, 15
and cannabis use 128.9
and depression, men 125.14
and football supporting 141.33
and human cloning 144.6
and gender differences 112.32–3
and mental health 141.34
mixed-faith 115.39
mixed-race 115.22–5
and women 112.31
relative poverty 110.21, 22–3
relaxation
and depression 125.39
and self-esteem 117.35, 37
and stress 100.29–30, 31–2, 34, 36–7
released (outdoor) GMOs 138.12
relief, feelings after bereavement 116.4, 19 religion
and abortion 126.1–3, 6
and the Census (2001) 94.3, 5–6, 28
and children's rights 120.2
and corporal punishment 132.11
and depression in older people 105.39
and euthanasia, 102.2, 8–9, 12–14, 17, 18
assisted suicide 102.17
and the killing of disabled babies 102.26
and food rules 94.10
funeral traditions 116.33–5
homosexuality and the Church 101.6, 15, 18, 29
and life expectancy 105.29
myths about 94.8–9
and terrorism 92.2–3, 6, 15–16; 94.10
and humanism 94.39
legislation 94.27–8, 29, 32, 35–6
and religious tolerance 94.26
religious discrimination 115.26
religious education see RE (religious education)
religious festivals 94.3–4
legislation on time off work for 94.35–6
religious groups
and disability 135.2
segregation 115.32
religious identity 115.5, 26
religious prejudice, perception of 131.3
religious tolerance 94.26–39
definitions of 94.26–7
and faith-based schools 94.30–1
and humanism 94.38–9

and Islamophobia 94.33
religiously motivated crime 115.27; 137.16
remembrance of the deceased 116.16–17, 20, 24
remembrance book 116.16
remembrance ceremonies 116.23
remembrance services 116.17
remote gambling 129.17–26
remote sensing satellites and surveillance 120.34
renewable energy 95.34, 36; 97.6–18, 26
advantages of 97.9
attitudes to 97.5
bioenergy 97.5, 6, 9, 11, 18
case for 97.1–2, 6–7
costs of 97.19, 38
defining 97.8–9
electricity from 97.4, 11, 37–8
future of 97.8–9
hydroelectric power 97.4, 5, 6, 12, 14, 38
and nuclear power 97.6, 7, 19, 21
sources of 97.4
types of 97.9
in the UK 97.13–14, 26, 39
see also energy efficiency; solar energy; wind energy
rent deposit schemes 130.29
rented accommodation
shortage 130.8
support services 130.29
Reporters without Borders 121.19, 21
reprimands, and youth crime 137.12
reproductive cloning 144.15
see also human reproductive cloning
reproductive rights 20.27–8, 35–8
disabled people 135.27
reproductive system, effects of eating disorders 127.5
reprogrammed cells 144.26
residential childcare, prohibition of corporal
punishment 132.15
resin, cannabis (hashish) 128.1, 3, 6, 23
seizures of 128.31
resistance training (exercise) 113.27
resources, definitions 111.4
respiratory health
and cannabis 128.18–19
lung cancer 128.17, 19, 28; 145.34
and passive smoking 145.29
responsibilities
and children's rights 120.1
young people 120.7–8
responsibility, encouraging children's 124.13–14
responsible drinking 143.26–7, 29
responsible tourism 109.18–39; 134.30
ecotourism 109.19–20, 38–9
definitions 109.27
glossary 109.23–5
and heritage sites 109.20–2
information on sustainable tourism 109.28–9
and working conditions in the tourist industry
109.30, 31
see also ecotourism
restaurants
and vegans 140.25

and vegetarians **140**.5
restorative justice **137**.12
restraint techniques in youth detention centres **120**.17
retail industry **98**.15–16; **107**.5
retail therapy **134**.13
retinoblastomas, and childhood cancer **60**.9, 11
retirement
    age of **105**.20, 27, 36; **107**.13
    attitudes to **105**.24
    early **105**.27
    and flexible working **105**.19–20
    and male depression **125**.15
    and the pension crisis **105**.19, 25
returnable bottles **111**.23
reusing waste **111**.4, 17
reverse anorexia **127**.19
Reynolds privilege **142**.27
RFID (Radio Frequency Identification) tags **82**.13–17, 35
    companies making or using **82**.13, 15–16, 35
    and crime **82**.17
    and data protection **82**.16
    defining **82**.13, 15
    disabling **82**.14
    identifying **82**.13–14
    media coverage of **82**.15
    possible consumer benefits of **82**.16–17
    and surveillance **82**.16
rhinoplasty, teenagers **117**.27
rice, GM contamination **138**.20, 31–4
rich-poor gap **98**.33–4
    global **110**.35
    UK **110**.13, 14, 16; **115**.32
rights
    in abortion
        of the fetus **126**.21–2, 27
        of men **126**.15
        of women **126**.21
    children's *see* children's rights
    consumer *see* consumer rights
    prisoners **137**.37–8
    same-sex partnerships and the law **101**.30–2
    to protest **121**.14
        about offensive material **121**.13
    young people **120**.1–22
    victims of crime **137**.28
    see also human rights
risk-taking and masculinity **112**.37
rivers
    and climate change **95**.21–2
    drying up of **76**.2, 35
    pollution **76**.4
        and freshwater supplies **76**.15
        paper mills **111**.32
    and species extinction **78**.10
road accidents **119**.4, 5, 28, 30–31
    and children **119**.5, 28, 30–31
    deaths **119**.4, 5, 28, 30
    and speed **119**.5, 30–31
    see also drink-driving
road building to ease congestion **119**.12

road charging **119**.35, 36
    congestion charging **119**.12, 34–5, 38
road safety **119**.4
    education **119**.5–6
    quiz **119**.6
road tax exemption, disabled people **135**.7
road traffic **119**.1
    increase **119**.11, 13, 29
    injuries, children **119**.5, 28, 30–31
    pollution *see* pollution and transport
    see also cars
role models
    boys **117**.23
    and self-esteem **117**.37
Roman Catholics *see* Catholic Church
Romanian labour, Germany **120**.30–31
Romans, sport and drugs **118**.23
rough sleeping **130**.9–12
    Scotland **130**.6
    see also homelessness
RSPCA Freedom Food mark **140**.29, 34
rubbish see waste
rural areas, poverty in **110**.25
rural views and mental well-being **117**.38–9

S

SAD (Seasonal Affective Disorder) **125**.4, 18, 37–8; **141**.35
sadness, feelings after bereavement **116**.19
safe houses *see* refuges
safe sex **101**.1, 17, 20
safety
    of abortion **126**.14
    and alcohol **123**.17
        drinks labelling **143**.30, 31, 32
    and cycling **119**.28
    in exercise **113**.28
    of genetically modified crops **138**.6–6, 24
    of goods, consumer rights **134**.20
    parents' fears **124**.13–14
    transport **119**.1
    and walking to school **119**.26
    at work **107**.31
    see also road safety
safety and the Internet **132**.33
    boundaries and regulation **104**.18
    chat and instant messaging **104**.35
    children and young people **104**.17–29
    computer and Internet addiction **104**.36–7
    filtering software **104**.19, 22, 23, 31
salaries
    graduates **139**.35, 36, 37
    teachers **139**.12
    see also earnings; wages
salmonella **88**.28
salt intake **88**.2, 7, 10, 16, 23, 26
    teenagers **123**.7
Samaritans **136**.29, 32, 37

and exam stress **123**.29–30
sanctity of life argument, and euthanasia **102**.2
sanitation
    in developing countries **76**.7, 8, 12, 17, 21
    and the right to water **76**.24
Satanism **94**.19
Sativex **128**.36, 37
saturated fats **88**.2, 22–3
savings
    attitudes to **74**.5
        children **74**.6–7
    and child poverty **110**.13
    lack of **110**.16
    levels of **134**.25
    and parents **74**.7
    savings accounts
        for children **74**.13
        and young people **74**.19, 24
    and teenagers **74**.8–9
    and young people **74**.15
Say Yes for Children campaign **120**.3
saying no **117**.3
scabies **96**.7
scalds, first aid **136**.23
scams **134**.26–9
schizophrenia **108**.2; **141**.4–5
    and assisted suicide **102**.6
    and cannabis use **128**.14–15
school bullying **122**.1–7; 11–12
    anti-bullying policies **122**.11, 18, 25
    and film violence **121**.28
    girls and young women **122**.10, 14, 15–16
    homophobic bullying **122**.3
    new school year **122**.12
    no-blame policy **122**.6–7
    peer support **122**.12
    racist bullying **122**.4–5
school holidays and bullying **122**.12
school leavers, lack of basic skills **139**.17
school leaving age **139**.1, 26
school meals **113**.5
    children's attitudes to food in school **123**.32
school uniform and gender equality **112**.10–11
schools
    abuse prevention programmes **108**.24–6
    academies **139**.14–16
    alcohol education in **143**.20
    behaviour problems **120**.16
    and children in developing countries **76**.13–14
    citizenship teaching **131**.36
    computers in **104**.11
    corporal punishment
        prohibion of **132**.15
        worldwide **132**.7
    drug tests **114**.26
    and disabled children **135**.24–5
    and ethnic minority children **115**.18, 19–21
    faith-based **94**.12–14, 28, 30–1, 38
    gender equality **112**.9–11
    and global citizenship **131**.37
    and integration **115**.29, 33

    and the Internet **104**.3
    journeys to **119**.25, 26–7, 29–30
    and litter **111**.8–9
    and mental health education **141**.37
    nature studies **117**.39
    and online learning **104**.9–10
    promoting physical activity **113**.6
    pupil-teacher ratio **139**.12
    and racism **115**.9, 19–20
    RE (religious education) **94**.9–10, 15, 31, 37
    and religious diversity **94**.39
    self-harm support **136**.11, 18
    sex education *see* sex education
    sexual abuse education **132**.27
    and sexuality
        and equality for gays and lesbians **101**.21–2
        homophobic bullying **101**.3, 18, 19, 20, 21–2,
            38–9
        and the repeal of section 28 **101**.18, 21, 22, 39
    single-sex **139**.11–12
    and special educational needs **135**.36–9
    sports **118**.3, 4
    statistics **139**.1
    teaching about money matters **74**.1, 6, 12, 32–3
    and weight measurement **127**.36
    young people and stress **100**.1
    young people's attitudes to **123**.2–3
    see also education; National Curriculum; primary
        schools; secondary schools
Schools Councils UK **131**.34
science, A-level choices **139**.21–2
scientific research, and animal experiments **103**.3
Scientology **94**.2–3, 17–18, 19
Scotland
    age of consent **133**.1
    children and gambling **129**.32–3
    Church of **94**.1
    and corporal punishment **132**.15, 16
    feelings of Scottish identity **131**.5
    homelessness **130**.5–6, 13
    improving employees' diet **113**.18
    self-harm among by older people **136**.20
    suicides **136**.34, 35
    teenage abortion **133**.2
    teenage pregnancy **133**.2, 5, 19
Scottish Episcopal Church **94**.1
scratchcards and under 16s **129**.12
screen violence, influence on children **121**.28, 33, 34,
    35
sea level rises **95**.1, 6, 7, 9, 11–14, 16, 25–6
Seasonal Affective Disorder (SAD) **125**.4, 18, 37–8;
    141.35
seasonal labour **89**.22–3
second-hand goods, consumer rights **134**.2
second-hand smoke *see* passive smoking
Second World War
    and family life **106**.1
    and terrorism **92**.7, 8
secondary schools
    curriculum **139**.5–6
    educational attainment

gender differences **112**.1, 8
see also schools
secularism
    and RE (religious education) **94**.9–10
    and religious discrimination legislation **94**.37–8
secure training centres, restraint techniques **120**.17
segregation **115**.28–32
segregation indices **115**.31–2
selective breeding **138**.12
Selective Serotonin Re-uptake Inhibitors (SSRIs)
    123.28; **125**.8, 10, 32
selenium
    in red meat **140**.12
    and vegetarian diets **140**.7
self-blame *see* blame, feelings of
self-censorship, broadcasters **121**.36–7
self-criticism **117**.6, 34
self-directed violence *see* self-harm; suicide
self-employment **107**.2
self-esteem **117**.1–9; **127**.24
    contributory factors **117**.4, 31–3
    definition **117**.1, 31
    and eating disorders **127**.2
    and green activities **117**.38–9
    healthy **117**.30
    high **117**.5, 31
        and criminality **117**.7
    improving **117**.1–2, 6, 33–9; **136**.3
        through learning and skills development **130**.35
    low, and bullying **122**.8
    questionnaire **117**.9
self-harm **123**.9, 36–9; **136**.1–26
    age of self-harmers **136**.4, 20
    asking for help **136**.12–13, 21
    case studies **136**.6, 15–16
    as coping strategy **136**.10, 25
    definition **136**.1, 4, 10, 17, 24
    and eating disorders **127**.10
    as expression of feelings **136**.10, 18
    in groups **136**.8–9
    and homophobia **101**.20, 22
    methods of **136**.1, 7, 9, 17, 26
    minimizing damage **136**.22–3
    myths about **136**.8–9
    older people **136**.20
    peer support **136**.18
    prevalence **136**.4, 7, 10
    prevention **136**.4–5
    prisoners **137**.37
    reasons for **123**.37; 1–2, 4, 5, 7, 10, 17–18, 20
    risk factors **136**.2, 10
    signs **136**.9, 10–11
    sources of help **123**.36–7; **136**.3, 12–13, 21
    self-help **136**.3, 19, 21
    stopping **136**.3, 21
    and suicide **123**.36; **136**.2, 9, 11, 24–6
    treatment **136**.11
    young people **136**.2, 4–19
self-image *see* body image
self-injury **136**.1–26
self-judgement **117**.4

self-poisoning **136**.26
self-reproach and traumatic bereavement **116**.11
separation
    effect on children **124**.33–4
    and male depression **125**.14
    and the process of divorce **106**.28
    see also divorce
separation from parents, children's rights **120**.11
September 11 2001 terrorist attacks **92**.8, 9, 11, 13, 14,
        16, 22
    and counter-terrorism
        in the European Union **92**.19, 21
        in the UK **92**.30, 31–2, 33–4, 35
    and Islamophobia **92**.36
serotonin **141**.9
    and eating disorders **127**.6–7
services
    and child labour **99**.2, 4
    and globalisation **98**.10, 23
Seventh-Day Adventist Church **94**.2
Severe Disablement Allowance **135**.5
Sex Discrimination Act (SDA) **112**.13
sex discrimination in employment **112**.13–14, 20
    see also glass ceiling, pay gap
sex education **123**.20; **133**.12–16
    age of children **133**.15
    aims **133**.13
    and attitudes to sex **133**.14
    and magazines **142**.28, 29
    role of parents **133**.12, 15
    about sexual abuse **132**.27
    and underage sex **123**.21
sex offenders **132**.22, 25, 26
    children as **132**.29, 30
    help for **132**.36–9
Sex and Relationships Education (SRE) **133**.12–13
sex segregation in training and work **112**.21–2
sex stereotyping *see* gender stereotyping
sex tourism **109**.5, 32, 35–6
sex work and street lifestyle **130**.12
sexual abuse **108**.5–6, 19, 29; **132**.1, 22–39
    and child domestic workers **99**.8, 9
    defining **101**.27; 1, 22
    effects **132**.4, 22, 23
    getting help **132**.23–4, 28
    and the Internet **132**.30, 31–2, 33
    misunderstandings about **132**.25–6
    recovering from **132**.28
    and self-harm **123**.37
    and sex education **132**.27
    signs of **132**.4
    and stress **100**.1, 2
    worldwide extent **132**.31
sexual abusers **132**.22
    children as **132**.29, 30
    help for **132**.36–9
sexual behaviour
    and early sexual relationships **123**.21
    and HIV **96**.12, 14, 16, 17
    and male depression **125**.14
    normal sexual behaviour of children **132**.29–30

and sexually transmitted infections **96**.9, 12
  teenagers **123**.19–21; **133**.1–3
  underage sex **123**.21
sexual exploitation of children **99**.1, 4, 16–18, 20–8
  case studies **99**.21–2
  harmful effects of **99**.16, 20
  and poverty **99**.16, 24
  and sex tourism **99**.17, 20, 23, 25–6
  teenagers **99**.20–2
  and trafficking **99**.3, 16, 17, 18, 20, 21, 24, 28
  see also child pornography; child prostitution
sexual harassment in schools **112**.11
sexual health clinics and STIs **123**.25
sexual imagery and TV watershed **121**.38
sexual intercourse
  and the conception of children **123**.22
sexual relationships, changing attitudes to **106**.20
sexual rights, disabled people **135**.27
sexual violence **137**.8
  see also rape
sexuality
  age of consent **101**.3, 27, 29
  and boys' culture **112**.34
  exploring **101**.1, 4
  labels and stereotypes **101**.1
  and the law **101**.1
sexually transmitted infections (STIs) **20**.27–8, 33–5,
      39–40; **96**.1–13; **101**.3, 4; **123**.5, 24–6
  avoiding **96**.1–2
  bacterial **96**.3, 10, 12
  chlamydia **96**.2–3, 4, 5, 8, 10, 12; **123**.26
  genital herpes **96**.3, 4, 6, 10, 12
  genital warts **96**.2–3, 4, 5–6, 12–13
  gonorrhoea **96**.2, 3, 4, 5, 8, 10, 12
  and HIV **96**.10, 12, 25
  increase in **96**.4
  pubic lice **96**.7
  and sexual behaviour **96**.9, 12
  symptoms of **96**.1, 5, 6, 7
  syphilis **96**.3, 4, 6, 8, 10, 12
  testing for **96**.1, 2, 3, 5, 6, 7, 10
  treatment of **96**.1, 5, 6, 7, 10
  trichomonas vaginalis **96**.6–7
  types of **96**.2
  in the UK **96**.2–3, 4
  viral **96**.12–13
  and young people **96**.3, 4, 8–9; **123**.3; **133**.2–3,
      12–13, 17
  see also Genito–Urinary Medicine (GUM) clinics
shantytowns **20**.17–18, 20
*Sharing Information with Disabled Children in the Early
      Years* **135**.21
sheep-goat chimera (geep) **144**.10
sherry, strength of **143**.1
Shinto **94**.19
shock as response to bereavement **116**.3–4
shopping
  addiction to **134**.13, 14
  and animal welfare **140**.31, 33
  and budgeting **74**.23
  and children **134**.12

and energy efficiency **97**.31–2
  from home **82**.36–7
  Internet **104**.5–8; **134**.15–16
  and money management **74**.17
  as social experience for women **134**.16
  and waste reduction **111**.16
  see also consumer rights; consumerism; consumers
sibling trouble **124**.18
Sicari (early Jewish terrorists) **92**.1, 6, 7
sickness absence **107**.6–8
Siemens Generation21 initiative **139**.22
Sikhs **94**.6
  and abortion and contraception **126**.2
  beliefs **94**.3
  and the Census (2001) **94**.3, 5, 28
  festivals **94**.4
  food rules **94**.10
  funerals **116**.34
  Golden Rule **94**.8
  and 'honour killings' **94**.30
  and RE (religious education) **94**.9
simple carbohydrates **88**.2
Singapore, littering laws **111**.10
singing, and building self-esteem **117**.33
single homelessness **130**.1–2
single mothers and poverty **110**.17
single parents *see* lone parents
single people
  and the cost of living **106**.13
  and the housing market **85**.7, 23–4
  lesbian, gay and bisexual **101**.9
  living alone **85**.2
  men **106**.3, 12, 20
  women **106**.3, 20
single-sex teaching **112**.4–6; **139**.11–12
sinsemilla (cannabis) **128**.1, 4
SIV (self-inflicted violence) *see* self-harm
skills shortages **107**.31–3
skin, effects of smoking **145**.30
skin cancer (melanoma) **60**.5, 18, 19–21
skunk (cannabis) **128**.2, 3–4, 13
  home growing **128**.3–4, 30–31
  mental health effects **128**.15
slander **142**.26
slavery **120**.29, 30–31
  and child labour **99**.1; **120**.18–19
sleep
  and exercise **141**.39
  and Internet addiction **104**.37
  and life expectancy **105**.29
  and mental health **141**.34
  and stress **100**.19, 27, 29
sleep eating disorder (SED-NOS) **127**.18
sleeper effect, smoking **123**.13
sleeping rough *see* rough sleeping
smacking children **132**.8–21
  arguments against ban **132**.14
  children's feelings about **132**.19–21
  defence of **132**.9–11, 14
  and human rights **132**.9, 12–13, 16–17
  perpetrators **132**.20

public opinion **132**.8, 18
small and medium sized businesses and workplace
	bullying **122**.36
smallpox vaccinations **92**.31
smart cards to record alcohol consumption **143**.29
'smarter justice' **137**.29–30
smoking **114**.5, 29
	age of smokers **145**.1
	anti-smoking advertising **145**.18–19
	ban on smoking in public places *see* smoking ban
	and cancer **60**.1, 2, 3, 14, 15–17, 27
	cannabis **128**.8
		effects of **128**.5, 18–19
	children **123**.11–13; **145**.2–3
		attitudes to smoking **145**.20
		starting smoking **123**.11, 13
	and coronary heart disease **113**.19–20
	costs of **145**.17, 38
		as deterrent **145**.3
	deaths from **145**.1, 4, 12, 22, 24
	giving up **145**.33, 35–9
		benefits **145**.27, 35
		numbers of people giving up **145**.1
		reasons for giving up **145**.15
	and health **145**.25–39
		benefits of giving up **145**.27, 35
		children **145**.2
		developing countries **145**.23
	and life expectancy **105**.2, 9, 30; **145**.21
	and litter **111**.9
	men **145**.21, 22
		and fertility **145**.32
	passive smoking **145**.2, 28–9
	sleeper effect **123**.13
	statistics **145**.1, 3, 4
	and stress **100**.19, 27, 31, 34, 35, 37
	withdrawal symptoms **145**.26–7
	women **145**.21, 22
		and fertility **145**.32
	workplace smoking ban **145**.14
	young people **123**.2, 8, 9, 11–13; **145**.3, 4
		influence of films on smoking habits **145**.9–10
		and the law **123**.12; **145**.3
		prevention **123**.12, 13
		reasons for smoking **145**.5
smoking ban (ban on smoking in public places)
	145.11–17
	effect on mental health staff **145**.39
	effect on mental health sufferers **145**.38–9
	effect on pubs **145**.13
	effect on tobacco industry **145**.16–17
	legal challenge **145**.15
	public attitudes **145**.13, 18
	and workplaces **145**.14
smuggled cigarettes **145**.17
soap bar (cannabis) **128**.1
soaps, TV
	and offensive language **121**.38
	and teenage drinking **143**.18–19
Social Attitudes Survey and disability **135**.30
social care services

and disabled people **135**.4
	expectations of **135**.18
	insuffiency **135**.20
	and older people **105**.6
social class
	and advertising **134**.8
	and Internet use **104**.3
	and mental health problems **141**.2
social exclusion **110**.8–9
social factors and gambling **129**.7, 29
Social Fund **135**.5
social gambling **129**.11, 18
social housing
	government strategy **130**. 16, 33
	shortage **130**. 8, 23
social identity theory and football support **141**.32–3
social inclusion effects of homelessness, children
		130.23
social inequality **110**.14
	and coronary heart disease **113**.19
social interaction and low self-esteem **117**.4
social isolation
	Asians **115**.37
	and self-harm **136**.18
social justice, and climate change **95**.16, 17
social life and self-esteem **117**.36
social mobility and education **139**.13
social model of disability **135**.1
social networking sites **142**.35, 36, 38
social pressures
	on athletes to use drugs **118**.29
	and eating disorders **127**.2
social responsibility **98**.6, 26, 29, 37–8
social security benefits *see* state benefits
social therapies for depression **125**.26
social tourism **110**.20
social workers
	and child protection **132**.3, 5
	and stress in young people **100**.2
	and workplace stress **100**.12
society, impact on gender development **112**.28
socio-economic groups
	and childhood obesity **113**.3
	and disability **135**.2
	and news awareness **142**.31
	and non-traditional families **124**.21
	and smoking **145**.1, 21
sodium intake, teenagers **123**.7
soft segregation **115**.28
Soil Association standards
	free-range eggs **140**.29, 39
	organic farming **140**.35
soil management **88**.14
solar energy **95**.34; **97**.2, 4, 6, 8–9, 10, 21
	costs of **97**.14
	and energy efficiency **97**.31
	market for **97**.14
	PV (Photovoltaics) **97**.8, 9, 12, 13, 38
	in the UK **97**.10, 13, 14, 26
solar radiation **95**.1, 2, 7, 8, 15
soldiers, suicides, Japan **136**.39

solicitors for court hearings **137**.36

solid fuels, as a source of energy **97**.4

solvent abuse **114**.21, 27–8

solvents and the law **114**.32

somatic-cell nuclear transfer (SCNT) **144**.1–2, 9, 26
    see also therapeutic cloning

somatic cells, and ageing **105**.1

soup runs **130**.31

soya products for vegetarians **140**.22, 23, 26

Spain, racism in football **118**.14

spam **82**.31–3, 36–7; **104**.30–1

spambots (spiders) **104**.30, 31

Special Educational Needs (SEN) **135**.36–9
    and mainstream schooling **135**.37–9

special schools **135**.36

specialist diplomas **139**.23–5

species boundaries **144**.12

Specs speed cameras **119**.17

spectators, pressure on athletes to use drugs **118**.23

speed (drug)
    and depressants **114**.17
    and ecstasy **114**.16

speed cameras **119**.4, 17, 18

speed limiters **119**.18

speed limits
    and active traffic management **119**.37–8
    raising **119**.4

Speedballs **114**.16

speeding **119**.3, 4, 8
    and pedestrian injuries **119**.5, 30–31

spending **134**.3–4
    on advertising **134**.7
    on credit cards **134**.24
    on education **139**.1
    on ethical products **134**.31, 32
    see also consumer spending

sperm cell creation from bone marrow **144**.29

spermicides **123**.23

spin, government **121**.17–18

spin doctors **131**.18

spinal damage, stem cell therapy **144**.21

spirits
    strength of **143**.1
    young people's drinking **123**.1

spoiled children as bullies **122**.9–10

sponsorship and women's sport **118**.21

sport
    benefits for young people **137**.29
    betting **129**.2
    and drugs **118**.23–39
    and inclusion **118**.12–22
    participation *see* participation in sport
    safety **113**.28
    trends **118**.1–11

Sport England **118**.1
    and planning applications **118**.5

sports facilities **118**.5–6

sports and gender equality **112**.11

spot weight reduction **113**.27

spread betting **129**.2

SSRIs (Selective Serotonin Re-Uptake Inhibitors)
    123.28; **125**.8, 10, 32

St John Patient Transport Service, Wales **135**.9

St John's wort, treatment for Seasonal Affective
    Disorder **125**.37–8

St Mungo's **130**.36–7

Staphylococcus aureus **88**.29

starchy foods **88**.5–6, 12

state benefits **110**.18
    for asylum seekers **89**.12, 13, 14, 19, 30, 38
    benefit problems
        and debt **130**.25
        and homelessness **130**.9, 12
    after bereavement **116**.30
    and child poverty **110**.4, 6, 7
    Child Tax Credit **74**.7; **110**.6, 7; **133**.33
    costs of incapacity benefit **100**.23
    Council Tax Benefit, lone parents **133**.35, 38
    disabled people **135**.3, 4, 5–6
        low take-up **135**.18
    Housing Benefit **133**.34–5
        problems, and homelessness **130**.9
    jobseekers' allowance **100**.23
    and lone parents **133**.33–6, 37, 38
        amount discrepancies **133**.36
        encouraging single parenthood **133**.32
    and older people **105**.5; **110**.19
    and students **74**.39
    Working Families Tax Credit **74**.7
    Working Tax Credit **133**.35
    see also disability benefits

state pension **110**.19, 20

state-sanctioned violence on children **120**.17

state-sponsored terrorism **92**.3, 7–8, 11

statutory homelessness **130**.2–3, 13

statutory rape **101**.27

Statutory Sick Pay **135**.5

steel cans recycling **111**.12, 23, 26

stem cell lines **144**.18
    personalized **144**.25

stem cell research **144**.2, 15–29
    ethical issues **144**.6, 17
    how it works **144**.16
    public attitudes to **138**.16; **144**.19
    timeline **144**.27–8, 33
    using hybrid embryos **144**.14

stem cell therapy **144**.17–18, 21–6, 28

stem cells **144**.15, 17–18
    from bone marrow **144**.21, 23

stepfamilies **124**.23–8, 39
    benefits **124**.25
    children's worries **124**.23, 26
    parents' worries **124**.27–8
    statistics **106**.3–4; **124**.23, 24, 25
    step-parenting **124**.39

stereotypes, gender stereotypes **108**.26

sterile-seed (Terminator) technology **138**.18

steroids *see* anabolic agents/steroids

stimulants **114**.1–2, 5, 29; **118**.36–7

stockbrokers, women **112**.26–7

stomach cancer **60**.4, 16, 17

Stop it Now! helpline (for sexual abusers) **132**.36
stop and search rights **128**.35
stopping cannabis use **128**.2, 10
stopping smoking *see* smoking, giving up
store cards **134**.22
storms, and climate change **95**.2, 5, 9, 11, 15, 25
Strategy Unit Drugs Project report **114**.11–12
street children **99**.1, 18–19
street drinking **130**.12
street homelessness **130**.9–12
    numbers **130**.9–10
    reasons for **130**.10–11
street lifestyles **130**.12
strength training **113**.23, 27
stress **107**.8, 18
    avoiding **141**.36
    and anxiety **100**.2, 21
    coping with **100**.27–39
    defining **100**.1, 5, 33
    and eating disorders **127**.16
    and exercise **141**.39
    factors determining degree of **100**.14–15
    'fight or flight' response to **100**.1, 14–15, 25, 28
    harmful effects of **100**.28, 38
    health benefits of the right sort of **100**.39
    and life expectancy **105**.10, 30
    and lifestyle **100**.19, 31–2
    men **112**.30
    positive and negative **100**.14
    reduction and self–esteem **117**.33
    signs and symptoms of **100**.1, 2, 5, 12, 28–9, 33, 35
    statistics on **100**.13, 19
    and workplace bullying **122**.30, 37
stress management **100**.32, 36
strokes **105**.3
    and depression **125**.5
    stem cell therapy **144**.22
structural adjustment **98**.3, 5, 7
students **107**.33, 35–6
    applying to university **139**.29–32
    health issues **123**.4–5
    and money matters **74**.1, 17, 19–22, 28–32, 34–9;
        134.24; **139**.34–5
    bank accounts **74**.1, 2, 17, 21–2, 29, 32
    budgeting **74**.2, 28, 30, 32
    bursaries **74**.32, 37
    costs of a university education **74**.38; **139**.34, 35
    course costs **74**.30
    credit cards **74**.3, 30, 32, 36, 37
    debts **74**.1, 3, 5, 19–20, 28–9, 31–2, 34–9
    disabled students **74**.39
    estimated average student expenditure **74**.29
    graduate starting salaries **74**.31; **139**.35, 36
    grants **74**.39
    hardship funds **74**.37
    living and study costs **74**.28, 30
    loans **139**.34
    overdrafts **74**.1, 21–2, 37
    and paid employment **74**.20, 29, 37
    part-time work **139**.35
    and parents **74**.19, 38

    and state benefits **74**.39
    tuition fees **74**.19, 20, 31, 37, 39
    university access funds **74**.39
    opinions on abortion for disability **126**.35
    statistics **139**.2, 32
style icons, boys' **117**.23
subsidies **98**.9, 10–11, 17, 31
substance abuse **114**.17
    and homelessness **130**.11, 20
    young people **123**.17
    see also alcohol; drugs
substance-induced cognitive disorder and ecstasy **114**.8
success, attitude to, and self-esteem **117**.8
suction termination (abortion) **126**.14
suicidal feelings
    after bereavement **116**.4
    children **123**.35
suicide **136**.27–39
    bereavement by **116**.8
    and cult members **94**.21
    and depression **125**.10, 22
    and euthanasia **102**.2
    impact on others **136**.28
    and the Internet **136**.37–9
    and the media **136**.37; **142**.30
    men **125**.15
    prevention
        how to help **136**.29
        initiatives **136**.31, 32, 36
    prisoners **137**.37
    reasons for **136**.27
    risk factors for **136**.25–6, 27, 30
    and self-harm **136**.2, 9, 11, 24–6
    statistics **102**.4; **125**.16; **136**.31, 33, 34, 35; **137**.8
    suicide pacts and the Internet **136**.39
    support for suicidal people **136**.27–8
        Samaritans **136**.29, 32, 37
    warning signs of **136**.11, 29, 30
    see also assisted suicide; attempted suicide;
        physician-assisted suicide (PAS)
Suicide Act and the Internet **136**.38
suicide bombers **92**.9, 15–16, 21
    profile of **92**.16
sulking, parental **124**.15
sulphur dioxide (SO2) emissions **119**.15
supercasinos **129**.14–16, 34
supermarkets
    and Fairtrade **134**.36
    and free-range eggs **140**.38
    and GM products **138**.26
    impact on communities **134**.38
    online grocery shopping **104**.5, 7
    and vegetarianism **140**.20
supermodels, and the wearing of fur **103**.36–7
supplements **118**.35
    and anti-doping rules **118**.33
    nutritional **118**.28
support groups
    abortion **126**.7
    alcohol abuse **143**.38, 39
    drug users **114**.19

families of drug users **114**.25
gamblers **129**.37
self-harmers **136**.3, 21
sexual abusers **132**.37–9
Support After Termination for Abnormality (SATFA) **126**.7
Supporting People grant funding programme **130**.34
surgery, and animal research **103**.3
surgical dilation and evacuation (abortion) **126**.10, 14
surveillance **82**.17–19; **120**.33–4
and facial recognition technology **82**.3
and the Government **82**.1–3, 22, 23
mass surveillance technologies **82**.1
and RFID tags **82**.16
workplace **120**.32–3
sustainable agriculture **88**.32–3
sustainable development **20**.24; **98**.38
definition **111**.4
and global water supplies **76**.17, 31
sustainable housing **85**.1, 9
in rural areas **85**.5
and sustainable communities **85**.32, 38, 39
sustainable tourism
and ecotourism **109**.38–9
funding bodies **109**.38–9
information on **109**.28–9
swearing on television **121**.38–9
Sweden, effects of smacking ban **132**.14
sweepstake scams **134**.26
sweets as food weakness **113**.14

T

t-GURTS **138**.18
tabloid newspapers **142**.8
tactile warning devices, cars **119**.19
tagging of asylum seekers **89**.36–7
tagging as a thinking error **117**.6
tai chi **81**.3, 14, 30, 31, 39
Take Your Daughters to Work Day **112**.20
talking
about deceased person **116**.15, 24–5
about feelings **141**.34
and the grieving process **116**.14–15
see also communication
talking therapies **125**.29–30; **141**.35
access to **125**.30–31
tariffs see trade barriers
taxation
on aviation fuel **119**.16
carbon tax on fuel **97**.25
Child Tax Credit (CTC) **110**.6, 7; **133**.33
overpayments to lone-parent families **124**.35; **133**.30
congestion tax **119**.34
contributions **89**.23, 30
fraud and error **133**.36
fuel taxes **119**.14, 24
gambling **129**.18

landfill tax **111**.3
and older people **105**.34
impact on rich and poor **110**.16
and same-sex partnerships **101**.30, 34
tobacco **145**.17
Working Tax Credit **133**.35
taxis and disabled people **135**.9
teachers
awareness of mobile bullying **122**.25
and homophobia in schools **101**.18, 22, 38–9
and ICT **104**.9
numbers of **139**.1, 12
salaries **139**.12
and stress in young people **100**.1
and workplace stress **100**.12
teaching materials, gender equality **112**.9, 10
team sports participation **118**.4
technological change, and workplace stress **100**.16
technology and bullying **122**.5, 19–26
teenage fathers **133**.25–7
teenage magazines **142**.28
teenage mothers **133**.18–24
education **133**.24
public attitudes to **133**.18, 21
single mothers **133**.28
teenage parenthood, long-term effects **133**.10
teenage parents **133**.20–27
see also teenage fathers; teenage mothers
teenage pregnancies **126**.30–31
and abortion **20**.30, 34; **126**.29; **133**.9
under 16s and confidentiality **126**.13, 28, 29
and adoption **133**.8–9
advice **133**.8
as biologically natural **133**.19
and family planning **20**.29–30, 34, 39
keeping the baby **133**.8
options **133**.8–9
planned **133**.20
and poverty **133**.20
and single parents **126**.31
statistics **126**.30–31; **133**.2, 4, 5–6, 12, 17
Teenage Pregnancy Unit **133**.4, 5
teenagers see young people
telephones
government surveillance of **82**.1, 22, 23
Telephone Preference Service **134**.20, 28
telephone sales and consumer rights **134**.20
workplace monitoring of calls **82**.27
television
advertising and children **134**.10, 12
alcohol advertising **143**.19, 20
and body image **117**.11–12
children **117**.22
and childhood obesity **113**.2
children's viewing **121**.27
and disabled people **135**.29, 32, 35
influence on young people **145**.6
as news source **142**.33
offensive language **121**.38–9
reality television, promoting racial understanding **115**.22

regulation **121**.36–7
   soaps
      and offensive language **121**.38
      and teenage drinking **143**.18–19
   watershed **121**.37, 38–9
   and women's sport **118**.21
   young people's viewing habits **142**.38
teleworking *see* homeworking
temporary accommodation **130**.9
   numbers of households **130**.5, 13–14
   and older people **130**.18
   Scotland **130**.5
tenancy support services **130**.29
terminally ill people
   and advance directives **102**.18, 34, 37
   and arguments against euthanasia **102**.13–14
   and assisted suicide **102**.6, 7, 9, 15, 16, 17, 27
   and freedom of choice **102**.30–1
   and hospice care **102**.3–4, 13, 28, 31
   and the law on euthanasia **102**.7, 8–9
termination *see* abortion
Terminator (sterile-seed) technology **138**.18
terrorism
   and aviation security **82**.3
   brief history of **92**.5–8
   deaths caused by **92**.34
   defining **92**.1, 10–12, 19
   deportation of suspects **120**.38–9
   different types of **92**.2
   fear of **92**.3–5, 13
   and guerrilla warfare **92**.12
   and identity cards **82**.2, 9, 10, 11; **120**.35; **131**.14
   and Islamophobia **131**.11
   London bombings **115**.27, 36
   media coverage of **92**.10, 23–4, 27, 28–9
   methods of attack **92**.9, 11–12
   Palestinian terrorist groups **92**.1, 2, 15–16, 20, 21
   and political violence **92**.10–11, 12
Tesco Mobile and mobile bullying awareness **122**.22–4, 25
testicular cancer **60**.5, 18, 26
   in children **60**.11, 12, 13
tetrahydrocannabinol *see* THC
text messages
   bullying **122**.5, 19, 21, 22–3, 24, 25
   preventing unwanted texts **134**.28
textiles recycling **111**.36
textured vegetable protein (TVP) **140**.19
Thalidomide, and animal research **103**.20
THC (delta-9 tetrahydrocannabinol)
   and cannabis strength **114**.37, 38; **128**.3
   effect on brain **128**.34
therapeutic cloning **144**.2, 15, 16, 26
   embryonic stem cells **144**.25
   humanist view of **144**.7
therapeutic exemption forms **118**.31–2
thermohaline circulation, and abrupt climate change **95**.18–19
Third World *see* developing countries
Thirteen (film) **121**.24–5
Thistle travel card scheme (Scotland) **135**.9

throat cancer **60**.15
thoughts
   and healthy self-esteem **117**.30
   and low self-esteem **117**.5, 6
thyroid cancer **60**.35
tidal energy **97**.2, 6, 12
timber recycling **111**.36
time limit for abortion **126**.12, 36–8
time management, and stress **100**.27, 29, 32, 36
tiredness and bereavement **116**.19
tissue cultures **103**.17, 19, 22
TNCs (trans-national corporations) **98**.4, 12–13
   agrifood TNCs **98**.28–9, 30
   and violation of human rights **98**.29
   and working conditions **98**.14, 17
tobacco **114**.5, 29
   advertising ban **145**.7
   chemical contents of smoke **145**.1
   consumption **145**.4, 22
   and the economy **145**.22–3
   and the law **114**.32
   and pharming of HIV drugs **138**.21–2
   plants **145**.25
   production **145**.22–3
   see also smoking
tobacco industry
   control of **145**.23, 24
   effect of smoking ban **145**.16–17
Today newspaper **142**.8–9
tofu **140**.6, 20
tolerance
   to alcohol **143**.7
   to drugs **114**.2, 5, 30
tomatoes, genetically modified **138**.14
torture
   evidence obtained under torture **120**.39
   victims **89**.18–20
totalitarian regimes, and terrorism **92**.7
tourism **98**.4
   and adventure travel **109**.9–10
   child sex tourism **99**.17, 20, 23, 25–6
   and climate change in the UK **95**.27
   in developing countries **20**.18
   and employment **20**.18
   global **109**.1–3
   independent holidays **109**.8–9
   Internet bookings **109**.16
   space tourism **109**.17
   UK travel trends **109**.4–5
   visits to the UK **109**.6
   young travellers **109**.11–15
   see also ecotourism; responsible tourism
tower blocks and racial segregation **115**.32
toxic chemicals
   and water pollution **76**.11
trade *see* international trade
trade barriers **98**.1, 2, 9, 22
   protectionism **98**.9, 10–11, 24
   subsidies **98**.9, 10–11, 17, 31
trade in endangered species **78**.16–17, 19–22
   and traditional medicine **78**.23

and the UK **78**.38–9
trade justice **98**.26–7, 31–2; **110**.32–3
trade unions **107**.31
    and globalisation **98**.13, 38
    and workplace stress **100**.11, 26
trading standards **88**.38–9
traffic *see* road traffic
traffic pollution *see* pollution and transport
trafficking **120**.28, 29
    and child labour **99**.1, 3, 4; **120**.18
    and the sexual exploitation of children **99**.3, 16, 17,
      20, 21, 24, 28
training
    disabled people **135**.15
    opportunities, racial discrimination **115**.14
    and starting a business **107**.4, 34
    vocational, girls **112**.21–2
    and workplace stress **100**.16
trains *see* railways
tranquillisers
    and cocaine **114**.16
    and the law **114**.32
    and speed **114**.17
transgender people **101**.7
transgenic bacteria **144**.11
transgenic technology *see* genetic modification
transport
    and disabled people **135**.7–9
    emissions *see* emissions, transport
    and energy efficiency **95**.5, 27, 28, 34; **97**.24, 25, 31
    environmental **134**.30, 32
    public attitudes to **97**.35, 36
    spending on **134**.4, 25
    trends **119**.1–16, 29–31
Transport 2000 **119**.32–3
Transport Innovation Fund **119**.38
transsexualism **101**.7
transvestism **101**.7
trauma memory **137**.9
traumatic bereavements **116**.10–12
travel
    documents **89**.33, 35
    ethical **134**.30
    and gender pay gap **112**.17
    and older people **105**.28
    and terrorism
      basic advice **92**.39
      fear of **92**.3, 4, 13
Travellers of Irish Heritage, and education **115**.18
treatment
    acne **123**.28
    alcohol abuse **143**.35, 38–9
    chlamydia **123**.26
    depression **113**.29; **123**.28; **125**.24–39
    drug addiction **114**.10, 18–19
    drug emergencies **114**.30
    eating disorders **123**.34; **127**.28–9
      binge eating **127**.16
      bulimia **127**.14
    manic depression **125**.19–20

    obesity **113**.12; **127**.34
      see also weight management
    post-natal depression **125**.17–18
    Seasonal Affective Disorder **125**.18
    self-harm **136**.11
treats and self-esteem **117**.37
trees
    effect of paper recycling **111**.32
    planting as way of remembrance **116**.17
tricyclics **125**.32
trips (drugs) **114**.29–30
truancy rates **139**.2
Truth Hurts report **123**.38
TVP (textured vegetable protein) **140**.19
Tween and Teen Trends, income survey **110**.10

U

U film classification **121**.29
UBE spam **104**.30
UCE spam **104**.30
UK
    armed forces recruitment age **120**.20
    and children's rights **120**.2
    drugs policy criticized **128**.38
    and European Union Charter of Fundamental Rights
      120.26–7
    gender gap ranking **112**.29
    genetically modified crops **138**.2–3, 5, 39
    Human Rights Act **120**.25–7
    identity cards **120**.35–6
    income inequality **110**.13, 14,16
    obesity **113**.2, 11–12
    online gambling market **129**.19, 20
    population, ethnic groups **115**.3
    poverty **110**.1–20
    and refugee children **120**.21
    supercasino **129**.14–16
    and world debt cancellation **110**.27–8
UK Life League **126**.25
UK Sport
    anti-doping programme **118**.26–7, 28, 30
    Drug Information Database (DID) **118**.31
    drug test statistics **118**.33–4
UK Youth Parliament **131**.29, 34
UN Convention on the Rights of the Child **120**.1–2,
    3, 4–6
    and school bullying policy **122**.11
    and child labour **120**.20
    and right to participation **120**.9–10
    and right to vote **120**.7
UN Conventions on drugs **128**.26
UN treaty on disability rights **135**.26
unauthorized absence (truancy) **139**.2
underachievement, black pupils **115**.19–21
underage drinking **137**.14
    and depression **125**.9
    ideas for reducing **143**.5, 29
    underage purchase of alcohol **143**.16, 20, 28

see also young people and alcohol
underage gambling **129**.1
    National Lottery **129**.11–13
    online gambling **129**.18, 25
    online poker **129**.25
    Scotland **129**.32–3
underage purchase of tobacco **145**.3
underage sex **123**.21
    abortion and confidentiality **126**.13, 28, 29
undergraduates *see* students
underground travel and disabled people **135**.9
underweight people, health risks **113**.16
unemployment **98**.19–20, 32, 37; **107**.10, 37–9
    and child poverty **110**.12
    and depression, men **125**.14–15
    disabled people **135**.3
    housing and environmental decline **85**.14
    and incapacity benefit **100**.23
    jobseekers allowance (JSA) **100**.23
    and older workers **105**.21
UNESCO International Convention against Doping in
    Sport **118**.27–8
unfair dismissal, investigation of claims of, and privacy
    rights **82**.26, 27
unhealthy diet and coronary heart disease **113**.20
UNICEF
    C8 event **110**.24
    Child Poverty in Rich Countries report **110**.4
    Childhood Under Threat report **110**.36
    and Convention on the Rights of the Child **120**.5, 6
Unification Church (Moonies) **94**.19, 20
uniformed organizations, benefits for young people
    137.26
uniforms, schools and gender equality **112**.10–11
union jack **131**.3–4
unions **107**.31
unipolar (endogenous) depression **125**.4, 10
uniqueness, and self-esteem **117**.1
Unitarianism **94**.2
United Reform Church **94**.2
units of alcohol **123**.16; **143**.1, 26
    awareness of **143**.11
    drink labelling **143**.30, 32
Universal classification, films **121**.29
Universal Declaration on Human Genome and Human
    Rights **144**.3
Universal Declaration of Human Rights **76**.24; **82**.4;
    89.6; **120**.23–5
universities
    admissions and exam stress **100**.7
    and animal rights activists **103**.15
    application numbers **139**.31, 32
    Bristol University, workplace travel plan **119**.32–3
    costs of a university education **74**.38; **139**.34, 35
    courses **139**.2, 29, 30, 38–9
    cults recruiting from **94**.24–5
    fees **139**.34
    funding **74**.19–20
    gender differences in performance **112**.1, 8
    and integration **115**.30
    post-qualification admission **139**.16

see also degrees; further education; students
unmarried parents **124**.22
upbringing and gender development **112**.35
Urban Spenders Survey **110**.15
USA
    and Convention on the Rights of the Child **120**.5
    gambling **129**.27
        underage online poker **129**.25
    and GM crops **138**.27
    income distribution **110**.35
    and mixed-race relationships **115**.24
    obesity **113**.9–10, 11
    overseas funding restrictions on abortion services
        126.19
    tobacco exports **145**.22
    worker exploitation **120**.30

V

v-GURTs **138**.18
vaccination
    and life expectancy **105**.2
    and organic farming **140**.35–6
vaccine damage compensation **135**.5
vacuum aspiration (abortion) **126**.14
value for money, and consumer rights **134**.2
values and Britishness **131**.1
vascular dementia **105**.37; **141**.6
vascular diseases and depression **125**.5
VCE (Vocational Certificate of Education) **139**.18
veganism **140**.2, 7, 25–6
    costs of **140**.25
    and health **140**.25
    and protein **140**.23–4
    and restaurants **140**.25
VegeMince **140**.19
vegetables *see* fruit and vegetables
vegetarian diets **140**.2, 6, 7
vegetarianism **88**.18; **140**.1–26
    definition **140**.1, 5
    eating out **140**.5, 25
    and food ingredients **140**.18
    and life expectancy **105**.29
    number of vegetarians **140**.20, 39
    reasons for becoming vegetarian **140**.1, 5, 8, 14
    and supermarkets **140**.20
Vehicle Excise Duty (car tax) and fuel efficiency
    119.24
vehicles
    adaptations for diability **135**.7
    recycling **111**.35
venison consumption **140**.15
verbal abuse **108**.1, 7
veterinary research **103**.10
Viagra and poppers **114**.16
vicarious liability for racism at work **115**.12
victimisation
    and racism **115**.7–8
        at work **115**.11–12

and religious discrimination **94**.28

and sex discrimination **112**.14

victims of abuse **108**.1

misunderstandings about **132**.25–6

treatment for **132**.5, 24, 28

victims of crime **137**.4, 9–10, 29

likelihood of becoming an offender **137**.14

racial identity **115**.10

and release of offenders **137**.28

rights **137**.28

victim personal statement **137**.31

young people as **137**.13, 17

video games

and children **121**.32–3

Video Recordings Act 1984 **121**.31

video sharing sites **142**.35

videos

and children **121**.26

regulation **121**.26, 31

see also films

violence

children as victims of **120**.17

and computer games **121**.33, 35

effect of corporal punishment **132**.10

disabled people as victims **135**.27

drug traffickers **114**.34

and male depression **125**.15

and masculinity **112**.37–8

in the media **121**.34

effect on children **121**.28, 33, 34, 35

physical restraint in youth detention centres **120**.17

see also physical abuse

violent crime

effects on victims **137**.9–10

statistics **137**.7–8

viruses, GM, to kill insects **138**.13–14

vitamins **140**.4

in meat **140**.12

Vocational Certificate of Education (VCE) **139**.18

vocational degree subjects **139**.38–9

vocational education, girls **112**.21–2

vocational qualifications **139**.4, 18

gender difference **112**.1; **139**.10

see also specialist diplomas

Voice UK **137**.28

volatile substance abuse (VSA) **114**.27–8

young people **114**.21

see also solvents

voluntary activity, England **131**.3

voluntary classification, video games **121**.33

voting **131**.16, 17, 18

eligibility to vote **131**.16, 18, 30

lowering voting age **120**.7–8; **131**.28, 29, 30

reasons for not voting **131**.22

voter apathy **131**.22

voter turnout **131**.19–21

wages

and child domestic workers **99**.9, 10

footballers **118**.11

minimum wage **107**.31

for students **74**.37

see also earnings; equal pay; incomes; salaries

waist measurement and obesity **113**.11, 15

Wal-Mart

commercial promotion to children **134**.11–12

unwillingness to employ overweight people **113**.17

Wales

age of consent **133**.1

National homelessness Strategy **130**.28

teenage pregnancy **133**.2, 5

walking

as alternative to car **119**.25

health benefits of **113**.31, 39; **119**.27

to school **119**.25, 26, 27

see also exercise; pedestrians

walking bus **119**.6, 26

war

effect on disabled people **135**.26

and terrorism **92**.10, 11, 13

on terror **89**.8

war-affected children **99**.32–5; **110**.36–7

and the effects of armed conflict **99**.33

help for **99**.34

problem of **99**.32

testimonials of **99**.33–4

warning letters, anti-social behaviour **137**.35

warranties, consumer rights **134**.18–19

waste

amounts **111**.5, 22, 38

as animal food **140**.17

collection **111**.6, 29

crime **111**.20

definitions **111**.1, 3–4

and energy generation **97**.37, 39; **111**.2, 3, 39

environmental impact **111**.1

history of **111**.5

incineration **111**.3, 6, 7, 15, 22

prevention **111**.16

reducing waste **111**.4, 17, 18

as a resource **111**.1

and water consumption **76**.1, 4, 19, 32, 36

in the workplace **111**.18

see also household waste; landfill; litter; organic waste; recycling

waste hierarchy **111**.1, 4

wastelands, and wildlife in London **85**.16–17

water abstraction, and wildlife **76**.34

water companies **88**.31

contact with schools **76**.1

multinational water corporations **76**.22, 23, 29–30

responsibilities of **76**.1

and water bills in the UK **76**.33

and water conservation **76**.36

water conservation **76**.1, 3, 22, 37–9

answering questions about **76**.36
in everyday life **76**.27
in the garden **76**.1, 36, 37, 38
in the home **76**.37, 38
investment in **76**.27
in schools **76**.39
and showers **76**.1, 27, 37, 38
and toilet flushing **76**.2, 27, 37, 38
water consumption
bottled water **76**.23, 27
and eco-systems **76**.2, 16–17, 19
groundwater sources for drinking **76**.7, 9, 12
and the importance of water quality **76**.9
lack of access to clean water **76**.8, 9
largest users of water **76**.36
per capita household water consumption by region
76.26
and population growth **76**.22, 29
reasons for growth in **76**.3, 5, 8
in selected countries **76**.7
statistics **76**.7, 9
and waste **76**.1, 4, 19, 32, 36
water requirements per person per day **76**.6
and water shortages **76**.21–2
water cycle **76**.2, 21
water management
and agriculture **76**.18
costs of **76**.33
dealing with the water crisis **76**.22, 26–8
government and planned policies of **76**.8–9, 17
and multinational water corporations **76**.29–30
pricing mechanisms **76**.22, 32
and privatisation **76**.22–3, 32
and wars over the ownership of water resources
76.22
water meters **76**.36, 38
water pollution **76**.1, 5, 10–11
causes of **76**.4, 7, 8, 9
in the developed world **76**.10–11
in developing countries **76**.4, 10
and global water supplies **76**.10–11, 15
and multinational water corporations **76**.29–30
statistics **76**.9
and water shortages **76**.36
water stress, calculating **76**.15–16, 17
water supplies **76**.15–17; **98**.26
and climate change **95**.1, 3, 7, 11, 12, 13, 15, 17, 26
financing the provision of **76**.31–2
and food production **76**.3, 4, 7, 18
and multinational water corporations **76**.29–30
and planned water management policies **76**.8–9, 17
and population growth **20**.6, 9, 13–14, 22, 23, 24
projected worldwide water use **76**.35
statistics **76**.1, 2, 4, 6, 8, 19, 20
and tourism **109**.30
and water as a human right **76**.24–5, 32
and water pollution **76**.10–11, 15
and water shortages **76**.15–17, 19, 21–2
water usage by sector **76**.3
and water users **76**.36
water vapour emissions

aircraft **119**.16
and global warming **95**.1, 8, 15
watershed, television **121**.37
erosion of **121**.38–9
wave power **97**.2, 6, 12
We the Children report **120**.3
wealth
children, UK **110**.10
and cultural poverty **110**.22–3
diseases of **110**.35
and obesity **113**.12
and segregation **115**.32
women **112**.19
weapons and violent crime **137**.7–8
weapons testing, animal experiments in **103**.1
weather patterns
and climate change **95**.2–3, 5, 7, 9, 11, 12, 15, 16,
25; **97**.1
abrupt **95**.19
websites
and bullying **122**.20, 21
and suicide **136**.37–9
wedding costs **134**.25
weddings rings, history of **106**.20
weight *see* body weight; obesity
weight concerns, young people **123**.1
weight loss rate **113**.27
weight management **113**.12, 31–2, 33; **127**.34
children **113**.7–8
and exercise **113**.34, 39
weight monitoring in schools **127**.36
weight perceptions, adults **113**.13
weight problems *see* obesity; underweight people
welfare reform bill **135**.23
welfare support *see* State benefits
West Antarctic ice sheet (WAIS) **95**.12, 13, 19
Western society and female body image **117**.16–17
whales
hunting **78**.6, 13, 14
watching **78**.13–14
wheelchairs **135**.7
Whitehouse, Mary **121**.36
wholegrain foods **88**.15
widowed people, suicide attacks by **92**.15
wild animals
in animal experiments **103**.6
as food **140**.17
and the fur trade **103**.38–9
wildflowers, threatened species in Britain **78**.36
wildlife
captive breeding **78**.22
conservation **88**.32, 34
and the exotic pet trade **78**.21–2
crime **78**.19, 38–9
illegal trade in **78**.21–2; **109**.39
killing of **78**.2, 4–5, 5–6
and the law **78**.16–17, 38–9
in London **85**.16–17
and new house-building in the south-east **85**.33
overcollecting **78**.22
and paper recycling **111**.32

and population growth **20**.6, 8–9, 14, 21, 22
rare species **78**.28
tourism **109**.29, 38
trade in live animals **78**.20–1
vulnerable species **78**.28
and water abstraction **76**.34, 36
see also conservation; endangered species; extinction
wills **74**.16
and lone parents **133**.38
Wilms' tumours **60**.9, 11
wind energy **97**.2, 4, 5, 6, 9, 21, 38
and climate change **97**.15
costs of **97**.16
energy available from **97**.5
new wind farm projects **97**.5
and noise **97**.17
numbers of wind farms **97**.11
offshore **97**.12, 16, 26
opposition to wind farms **97**.12
public attitudes to **97**.16
top myths about **97**.15–17
turbines **97**.5, 15, 17, 38
in the UK **97**.13, 26
wind power **95**.29, 34
wine
consumption, young people **123**.1
health benefits **143**.4
strength **143**.1
winter deaths, older people **110**.19
withdrawal from drugs **114**.5
withdrawal symptoms
cannabis **128**.15
gambling **129**.30
nicotine **145**.26–7
witnessing bullying **122**.1–2
womb cancer **60**.5
women
and abortion
decision-making **126**.16
rights **126**.21
views on abortion time limit **126**.36, 37–8
and ageism **105**.16
and alcohol
and heart attack risk **143**.7
pregnant women **143**.3, 25, 27, 33–4
and body image *see* body image, women
and cancer **60**.3, 4, 5, 27
cervical cancer **60**.5, 14, 16
lung cancer **60**.15
childless **20**.26
in construction industry **112**.25
in developing countries **20**.2, 3, 9, 20
disabled, violence against **135**.27
discrimination against older women **105**.16, 21–2
and divorce **106**.26, 31
employment prospects **107**.32
equality and child labour **99**.12
and exercise **113**.23, 27, 28
and family planning **20**.25, 26, 27, 29–30
and fertility *see* fertility; infertility
and the future of work **107**.12

and gambling **129**.21, 34
online gambling **129**.27
gender pay gap **107**.13, 25, 26; **112**.16–17
glass cliff/glass ceiling **107**.9; **112**.15–16, 20
graduate salaries **139**.36
and higher education **112**.8
and HIV/AIDS **96**.20, 24–5, 29, 30–1
and homelessness **130**.15
and the Internet **104**.12
job satisfaction **112**.22–3
life expectancy **105**.2, 9, 19
low self-esteem **136**.2
maternal mortality **20**.25, 28, 29, 30, 36, 37, 39
maternity leave **107**.16, 21
and mental ill-health **141**.1
and online shopping **134**.16
and part-time working **107**.17
post-natal depression **125**.4, 17–18
and poverty
global **110**.22
in the UK **110**.11, 17–18, 19
pregnant women **88**.7
and prison **137**.39
and sexually transmitted infections (STIs) **96**.3, 9
single **106**.3, 20
and smoking **60**.27; **145**.21, 22
sperm creation **144**.29
in sport **118**.18–20, 21–2
and stress **100**.13
frequent worrying **100**.19
and suicide **136**.33, 35
suicide attacks by **92**.15
violence against **137**.8
wealth **112**.19
working mothers **107**.26
working in the tourist industry **109**.33
see also girls and young women; infertility; mothers;
pregnancy; working mothers
women in the workforce **112**.12, 20
equal pay *see* equal pay
and the 'glass ceiling' **112**.15–16, 20
managers **112**.18
non-traditional careers **112**.21, 25–7
and the pay gap **112**.16–17, 20
and the UK labour market **112**.12
see also working mothers
wood recycling **111**.36
woodland burial grounds **116**.39
words to describe racial identity **115**.4–5
work
absenteeism and obesity **113**.17
effects of cannabis use **128**.14
exploitation of workers **120**.28–31
gambling at work **129**.22–4
see also child labour; employment; slavery
work experience and specialist diplomas **139**.24, 25
work and gender *see* gender and work
work-family balance **112**.37, 38
work-from home scams **134**.27
work-life balance **107**.6, 14, 16
and age **105**.24

see also hours of work
Workability project **135**.15
workaholism **107**.29
working abroad **107**.3
working conditions **98**.4, 13, 14, 17, 25–6
    in the tourist industry **109**.30, 31, 32
working hours *see* hours of work
working mothers **107**.26
working parents **107**.21–2, 24–5, 26
    effect on families **124**.1, 21
    role of father **124**.7–8, 11
Working Tax Credit **133**.35
workophiles **107**.2
workplace
    and disabled people **135**.15
    dismissals
        reasons for **82**.28
        unfair **82**.26, 27
    drug testing **128**.20
    and energy efficiency **95**.32
    gambling **129**.22–4
    gender equality, and men **112**.36–7
    and healthy eating **113**.18
    and Internet addiction **104**.37
    and personal emails **104**.15
    and privacy rights **82**.25–30
        and CCTV **82**.26, 27
        company policies on electronic communications **82**.30
        European-level regulation of **82**.28
        personal information **82**.30
    racism **115**.11–14
    segregation and pay gap **112**.17
    smoking ban **145**.14
    surveillance **120**.32–3
    travel plans **119**.32–3
    waste **111**.18
    working conditions **98**.4, 13, 14, 17, 25–6
workplace bullying **122**.27–39
    anti-bullying policies **122**.39
    avoiding **122**.35
    defining **122**.27, 28, 37
    effects **122**.30, 31, 33, 37–8
    and harassment **122**.30
    responses to **122**.27, 31–2, 33, 37–8
    signs **122**.27, 28–9, 37, 39
    and small businesses **122**.36
    support **122**.31–2, 38
World Anti-Doping Agency (WADA) **118**.25, 27
World Anti-Doping Code **118**.27, 31–2
World Bank **98**.1–2, 3, 7–8
    organisational structure **98**.7
    origins **98**.7
    project failure rate **98**.7
    and world debt **110**.27
World Cup, effect on mental health **141**.23
World debt **110**.27–8
World food supply, and GM crops **138**.9, 10, 34–5
World Fit for Children, A **120**.3
World Fit for Us, A children's forum **120**.3
World Summit for Children **120**.3

world trade *see* international trade
World Trade Organisation (WTO) **88**.33
    enforcement of trade rules **98**.27
    and global water supplies **76**.5, 23
    and globalisation **98**.3, 9–10, 17, 21–3
    and the liberalisation of water **76**.29
World Wide Web (WWW) **104**.2
    browsers **104**.2
    pharming websites **104**.33–4
    phishing websites **104**.32–3
worries, young people **123**.2–3

Y

Y Vote Mock Local elections **131**.27
Yahoo and Chinese censorship **121**.19
yoga **81**.3, 30, 39
    and exam stress **100**.5
young children
    gender differences in achievements **112**.7
    obesity **113**.3
young offenders
    custody **137**.12, 15, 19
    risk factors **137**.13, 14, 16–17
    and street homelessness **130**.11
    types of crime **137**.11–12, 16
young parents and non-traditional families **124**.20–21
young people
    and abortion **126**.13, 17–18, 28–9
        confidentiality **126**.13, 28, 29
        telling parents **126**.28, 29
        views on abortion for disability **126**.35
    affordable housing for **85**.3–4
    and age discrimination **105**.16, 24
    attitudes to biotechnology **138**.16
    attitudes to global poverty **110**.24
    attitudes to Islam and terrorism **92**.36
    attitudes to marriage **106**.5
    attitudes to mental ill-health **141**.25
    attitudes to work **105**.23
    bereavement support **116**.28
    and cannabis
        behavioural effects **128**.16
        possession **128**.27
        cannabis use **128**.6, 21
        education about risks **128**.28
        penalties for use **128**.9
    as carers **135**.10–12
    and child pornography **132**.30
    and citizenship *see* young people and citizenship
    and contraception **123**.22; **126**.23
    and crime *see* young offenders; youth crime
    and criminal justice system **137**.17, 19
    and debt **134**.24
    and depression **123**.27–8; **125**.8, 9
    in developing countries **20**.10–11, 33–4, 40
    and divorce **124**.29–30, 34
    and drug abuse **114**.20–28; **123**.14
        and driving **114**.23–4

and eating disorders **123**.33–4

and emotional problems **123**.10

fear of **137**.26–7

and funerals **116**.23

and gambling **129**.1

    gambling addiction **129**.25, 31, 32–3

    National Lottery **129**.11–13

    signs of problem gambling **129**.38

    views on gambling **129**.13

and grief **116**.19–28

health-related behaviour **123**.1–3

and healthy eating **88**.4

and HIV/AIDS **96**.17, 24–9, 38

homelessness *see* homeless young people

house prices and first-time buyers **85**.6, 7

and identity (ID) cards, opposition to **82**.7

and the Internet **104**.3–5, 9–11, 13, 17–29

and justice system **120**.1–2, 12–13

media habits **142**.38

media representation **142**.15

and mental health **123**.9; **125**.16

and mental illness **141**.25

and money matters **74**.1–4, 14–17

    attitudes to money **74**.2

    budgeting **74**.2, 3, 14–15, 23

    credit cards **74**.15, 16

    debt **74**.1, 2, 15, 16, 23–4

    and insurance **74**.2, 15

    paying bills **74**.2

    pension planning **74**.1–2

    savings **74**.15

    teenagers **74**.8–9

negative representation of **137**.24, 25

news awareness **142**.32

and nutrition **123**.1, 6–7

and obesity **123**.31

parenthood *see* teenage parents

parenting teenage children **124**.16–17

and the police **137**.14

and politics *see* young people and citizenship

poverty and mental illness **141**.22

and pregnancy *see* teenage pregnancies

and religion **94**.6–7

rights **120**.1–22

and safety **137**.20

and self-harm **123**.36–9; **136**.2, 4–19

and sex **123**.19–21

as sex abusers **132**.29, 30

and sex education development **133**.15–16

sexual exploitation of teenagers **99**.20–2

sexual health **20**.33–4, 40

and sexuality

    coming out **101**.11–13, 17

    exploring **101**.1

    and the law **101**.3, 27

and sexually transmitted infections (STIs) **96**.3, 4,

    8–9, 25; **123**.25–6; **133**.2–3, 12–13, 17

as single parents **126**.31

and smoking **123**.11–13; **145**.1, 2–6

    influence of films **145**.9–10

    nicotine patches **145**.20

and sport **118**.2

  and suicide **123**.35; **136**.27–8

teenage girls

    body image **117**.20–21

    and domestic violence **108**.29

    eating habits **117**.20

    plastic surgery **117**.26–8

as victims of crime **137**.13, 17

voting rights **120**.7–8

worry about getting older **105**.8

young people and alcohol **123**.1–2, 9, 14–19

  alcohol misuse **143**.29, 37

  alcohol consumption **143**.2, 5, 15, 20, 37

  drinking habits **123**.1–2, 19; **143**.2, 5, 15–17, 21, 37

  eating problems **127**.20–21

  effects of **123**.15

  exceeding daily benchmarks **143**.8

  getting help **123**.14

  and HIV **96**.26

  influence of others **143**.17

  influence of television soaps **143**.18–19

  and the law **123**.16; **143**.2, 17

  obtaining alcohol **143**.16, 17, 20, 28

  problems **123**.18–19

  proposals to cut underage drinking **143**.5, 29

  risks **123**.14

  safety information **123**.16, 17

  statistics **123**.1–2

  under-age purchase of alcohol **143**.16, 20, 28

young people and citizenship **131**.26–39

  civic involvement **131**.31–2

  and decision-making **131**.28

  and the EU **131**.39

  feelings of exclusion **131**.26

  involvement in politics **131**.35

  and mock elections **131**.27

  political interest **131**.28, 31, 32, 35

  political party support **131**.32

  views on citizenship **131**.31–2

  youth councils **131**.33–4

  youth parliaments **131**.29, 33–4

Young People into 2006 report **123**.1–3

Young People's Parliament (Birmingham) **131**.34

Young Scot **131**.34

Your Shout About Africa survey **110**.24

youth detention centres, restraint techniques **120**.17

youth councils **131**.33–4

youth crime **137**.11–27

  causes **137**.13, 14

  and education **137**.13

  extent of **137**.11, 14, 16

  and mental health **137**.13

  statistics **137**.11, 16

  types of offence **137**.11–12, 16

  and victimization **137**.13

  see also young offenders

youth custody **137**.12, 15, 19

Youth Inclusion Programmes (YIPs) **137**.12

Youth Inclusion and Support Panels (YISPs) **137**.12

youth justice **120**.12, 13

  statistics **137**.19

First published by Independence
PO Box 295
Cambridge CB1 3XP

© Independence 2007

ISBN 978 1 86168 418 9

Layout by Hart McLeod

Printed in Great Britain
MWL Print Group Ltd